ECCLESIASTES

God's Game Plan for Life

A six-week line-by-line study of Ecclesiastes

A Wells of Truth

Small-Group Study

L.B. Brown

Printed in the United States of America
First Printing, 2021
ISBN 978-1-941749-91-3
4-P Publishing
Chattanooga, TN 37411

Some questions are taken from Lesson Maker 8 software

Contact Coach Laura

www.coachlaurabrown.com

coachlaurabrown@gmail.com

Download a FREE Group Leaders guide

https://www.coachlaurabrown.com/free-downloads

GAME PLAN

Ecclesiastes

God's Game Plan for Life

INTRODUCTION AND INSTRUCTIONS

I am delighted you chose this journey through God's word. I pray you be enriched, empowered, and enlightened. To get the most out of this study, I want to give you a few instructions and study helps.

Items Needed:

1. You will need a bible for this study: I use the **NASB,** but any good study version will do. I don't recommend modern language versions (i.e., the Message) for the study portion. They are helpful when comparing passages, but otherwise, I recommend a study bible (NASB, KJV, NKJV, ESV are best, in my opinion). Whatever you have, I hope you don't mind marking/coloring in it! For those who don't have a NASB or don't want to mark in your bibles, I have included all the necessary scriptures and cross references used during this study in the appendix. By using the included appendix, you will save time during your study.

2. That brings us to our second item—colored pencils/pens for marking your Bible.

Study Guidelines:

1) You should plan for at least **30-40 minutes** each day. You may want to spend more time than that and add your own study items. The point is to make it a daily habit. If completing this study with a group that meets weekly, **DO NOT** wait until the last minute and cram it all in. You will get the most out of this study if you go at a steady pace daily. The seventh day is for group discussion.

2) The *"Time Out boxes"* on the pages are helpful but **optional.**

3) As you read, remember to ask the **5 Ws and the H**:

   - **Who** are the main characters?
   - **What** is the passage about?
   - **When** does it take place?
   - **Where** does it take place?
   - **Why** is it being said or done?
   - **How** did it happen?
   - **How** does this apply to me?
   - Think about the **ABCs** of self-management: attitude, behavior, or corrections needed.

- The section labeled *"run the play"* is a guide for practical application.

4) **Mark Key Words** - A keyword is any word or phrase that an author repeatedly uses to make a point or convey their message. When marking keywords, be sure to mark their synonyms also. You should use colors, symbols, or any combination that you will remember consistently throughout the bible. I'll give some suggestions.

5) **Interpretation** - **BEFORE** you decide what it means, make sure you are interpreting it in its context. Read various versions to assist with this. Use commentaries only **AFTER** you have done the work of interpretation to compare thoughts. If you come to a difficult passage to understand, you may want to annotate and come back to it when you have time to do a deeper study or bring the question to your group discussion.

6) **Prayer** - Last but certainly not least, always pray **BEFORE** reading. Ask God to show you what He would have you to get out of your reading.

7) **Understanding** - Always remember, the most important thing about this study is **understanding** what you read. If you don't complete all the questions or exercises, don't get discouraged. The main thing is to read the assigned text in your bible. If you find yourself crunched for time on some days and have to choose between answering the questions or reading the text, **always** choose to read the text.

How This Study is Designed

This study is designed using a few sports terms. Take note of the symbols/graphic images used to alert you of the action you are to take. The first week of study includes reminders about image meaning, and after that, you should start to recognize them. Look at the following symbols and their instructions:

 **The Locker Room** is the place to suit up in prayer and get equipped for the game. The locker room will tell you what items you need from the appendix to assist you in this study.

 **Warm Up** - This is the place to get yourself "loosened up" and ready to engage with the text. You will answer general questions that will relate to the passages you will be reading. You will also read and mark the text during this time.

Sideline - This is where you observe and get instructions on how to execute the play during the game. You will answer <u>simple</u> observation questions about the text.

Run the Play - This is where you actively engage with what you have read and connect it with your life. Running the play requires you to expand your thinking as you apply what you observed during your time on the sideline.

Instant Replay - This is where you decide which verse you'd like to commit to memory. You can choose to create a short saying to help you remember what you have learned.

Halftime - This is a great time to take a pause and ponder what you have just learned in the first two quarters of "the game." Are there any questions that you have which you'd like to explore? Check out a few of the **Time Out** boxes, which are scattered throughout the workbook if you like. After halftime, we switch chapters.

Time Out - These boxes contain tidbits of additional information. Most of them are optional and designed to give you a deeper understanding of what you are studying. When necessary, you will be instructed to read the information within them.

Athlete Interview - This is your chance to share how you would respond to a specific idea or question. The questions are designed for you to put together all you have studied to share with others.

Game Highlights - This is where you will close out your week with prayer, thoughts, or questions you'd like to explore further. Take this time to review your life and how it lines up with the Word of God.

Although this workbook is packed with valuable information and tools to assist you in your study, you won't find a great deal of assistance in the form of my thoughts or opinions. I desire to equip you well enough to form concrete thoughts through your own study. I read the following saying somewhere, and it has been my guide and motto as a teacher. It simply stated, "A great teacher is able to tell students where to look without telling them what to see."

Well, it's game time…let's head to the stadium of God's word. What is our first stop? The Locker Room, of course.

WEEK ONE

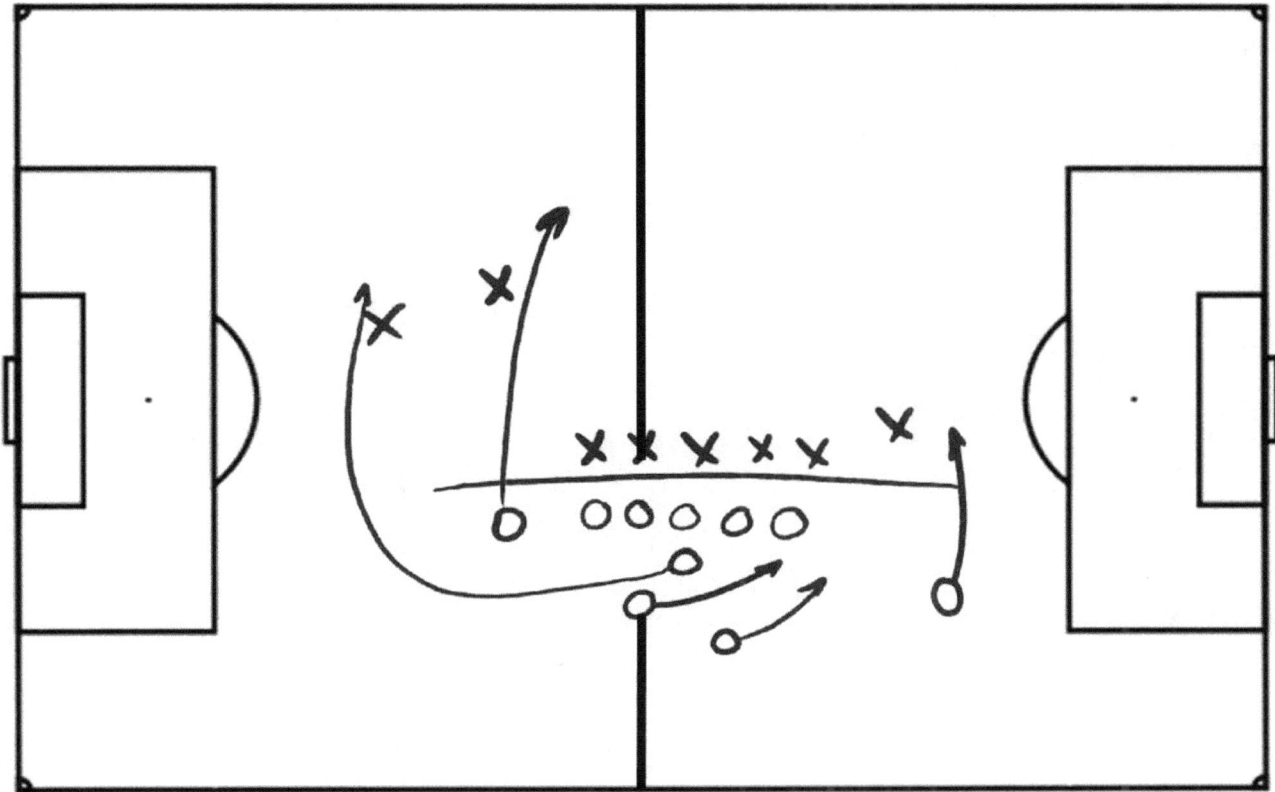

WHAT'S THE POINT?

Ecclesiastes – God's Game Plan

Day 1

The Locker Room *(place to suit up in prayer and get your equipment for the game)*

You will need:

☐ Ecclesiastes Chapter One (Appendix A)

☐ Vanity Chart (Appendix B)

☐ Under the Sun Chart (Appendix C)

☐ Week one Cross Reference Scriptures (see Appendix D)

Warm Up *(the place to get yourself "loosened up" and ready to engage)*

Always remember to begin each day with prayer. Pray that Holy Spirit gives you an understanding of what you read. Pray that you will uncover fresh nuggets from God's word. Pray for change within your heart and mind.

• What are some things that make your life worth living?

• What is the difference between being unsatisfied and dissatisfied?

• If money was not a concern, what are some meaningless things you might buy or do?

Read Ecclesiastes 1 all the way through to get an overview of the chapters. We will approach each new chapter in this way. Think about who, what, when, where, why, and how **(5 Ws and H).**

Now, go through and mark the following **Key Words:** *vanity* (the words *futility* and *striving after the wind* and *emptiness* will be marked the same way in later chapters). Read again and mark the phrase *under the sun* and *under the heaven*. Also, mark *wisdom* and *folly.* In the coming weeks, you will be keeping charts of what Solomon describes as "vanity" and what he has noticed taking place "under the sun/heaven." As you come across these words and phrases, place them in the appropriate chart. When this study is complete, you will have an at-a-glance overview of these subjects.

Day 2

First Quarter –Ecclesiastes 1:1-11

Sideline *(the place where you observe and get instructions on how to execute the plays during the game. You will be answering basic observation questions about the text. Summarize your answers in one or two short sentences).*

• What do you learn about the author in chapter 1? Ask your 5 Ws and H?

• What general statement did Solomon make about life? (1:2)?

•

• What question did Solomon ask? (1:3) Remember to start your chart for the phrase *under the sun* and the word *vanity.* Note that the words *emptiness, striving for the wind,* and *futility* mean the same as vanity.

Vanity

Strong's H1892 - *hebel* - breath, vapor

References to vanity appear often in the Bible, and the word has a variety of meanings such as meaninglessness, wickedness, falseness, idolatry, worthlessness and futility. The way we typically use this word today to mean "boastful" is actually not that common in the Bible.
eHow.com

• How did Solomon use the cycle of nature to emphasize his statement in vs. 2? (1:4-7)?

• What does he say about man's search for satisfaction? (1:8-10)?

Read more:
http://www.ehow.com/about

• What does he say will be forgotten? (1:11)?

Ecclesiastes – God's Game Plan

Run the Play-Application *(this is where you actively engage with what you have read and begin to connect it with your life.)*

- What do you find meaningless about life?

- How limited was Solomon's understanding when compared to what you know now?

- How would you respond to Solomon about his statement in verse 11?

Day 3

Second Quarter – Ecclesiastes 1:12-18

Sideline

- To what did Solomon devote himself? (1:12-13)?

- What role does wisdom play in his pursuit? (1:12)?
    - Look at the following verses (see Appendix D):
        - ☐ Pr. 1:7, 2:6; 9:10; 15:33
        - ☐ 1 Cor. 1:18-25

- How did he feel about this task (1:13)?

- What conclusion did Solomon reach about everything he had seen and done (1:13-18)?

Run the Play

- Why do you think he felt it was a burden to search these things out?

- In what way does increased wisdom and knowledge bring increased sorrow and grief?

- Why was Solomon so dissatisfied with life? Have you ever felt this way? Why?

- In what ways do you see people living in this kind of despair and hopelessness today? What would you say to them?

- What is one meaningless activity you need to eliminate from your life or reduce the amount of time you spend doing?

 Instant Replay *(This is where you decide which verse you'd like to commit to memory. Which one stood out as you were studying the passage?)*

Memory Verse:

 *This is a great time to take a pause and ponder what you have just learned in the first two quarters of "the game." Are there any questions you have which you'd like to explore? Check out a few of the **Time Out** boxes scattered throughout the workbook. When you return, we will switch chapters.*

Day 4

Locker Room

You will need:

☐ Ecclesiastes Chapter 2 (Appendix A)

☐ Vanity Chart (Appendix B)

☐ Under the Sun Chart (Appendix C)

☐ Cross Reference Scriptures (Appendix D)

Warm Up

• What priority do you think a person should give to leisure and fun?

Read through Ecclesiastes 2 to get an overview. Reread it, mark the same keywords from chapter one, and include the words *labor, fate* (you can draw a small red clock). Mark references to *God* (remember pronouns also). If you don't already have a preferred marking for *God,* you can use a purple triangle with a yellow highlight.

The Pleasure Principle

Hedonism (heed -n-iz-uhm)

In ethics, the doctrine that pleasure or happiness is the highest good in life. Some hedonists, such as the Epicureans, have insisted that pleasure of the entire mind, not just pleasure of the senses, is this highest good.

Epicureans

Followers of Epicurus (who died at Athens B.C. 270), or adherents of the Epicurean philosophy (Acts 17:18). This philosophy was a system of atheism, and taught men to seek as their highest aim a pleasant and smooth life. They have been called the "Sadducees" of Greek paganism. They, with the Stoics, ridiculed the teaching of Paul (Acts 17:18). They appear to have been greatly esteemed at Athens.

Bible Dictionary

Ecclesiastes – God's Game Plan

Day 5

Third Quarter – Ecclesiastes 2:1-11

Sideline

- What did Solomon say about his pursuit of pleasure (2:2)?

- List some ways Solomon sought pleasure (2:3-9)?

    o What advantage did he have over the average person in his pursuit of pleasure?

    o In what ways can wealth be harmful or meaningless to a person?

        ▪ Read Pr. 30:7-9 (Appendix D)

- What was the result of Solomon's search for pleasure (2:10-11)?

Run the Play

- What are some meaningless things people pursue to find satisfaction?

- In what ways can you seek to find true satisfaction and enjoyment from your life's pursuits and avoid or minimize frustration?

- Are there any areas of your life that you need to re-prioritize in light of this week's study?

Ecclesiastes – God's Game Plan

Day 6

Fourth Quarter - Ecclesiastes 2:12-26

Sideline

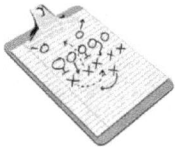

- What was The Preacher's next pursuit? (2:12)

- What did he discover about the wise man and the fool? (2:13-16)

  - How did that discovery make him feel? (2:17-20)

- Why did he come to feel this way? (2:21-23)

> *Memory-*the knowledge or impression of somebody retained by other people after that person's death
>
> *Legacy-*something that is handed down or remains from a previous generation or time

- What does he conclude about making work a priority? (2:24-26)

- What role should God play in the enjoyment of our labor and search for wisdom? (2:24-26)

Run the Play

- Considering the verses you read in Proverbs and I Corinthians on day 3, with what points of Solomon's assessment of life do you agree or disagree?

- How would you respond to the idea that ALL labor and wisdom are vanities?

- Have you given any thought to how you will be remembered?

- If a movie was of your life, who should get the starring role? Why?

- What are you building now that will have a lasting impact after you die? Are you creating a *Memory,* or are you building a *Legacy?* What is the difference?

Instant Replay

Memory Verse:

Game Highlights: *(this is where you pray and ask the Lord to help you align your life with His word. Are there any areas you want to see changed in your life? Thank Him for His wisdom and ask for insight into pursuing those things He desires for you. Pray His word right back to Him.)*

WEEK TWO

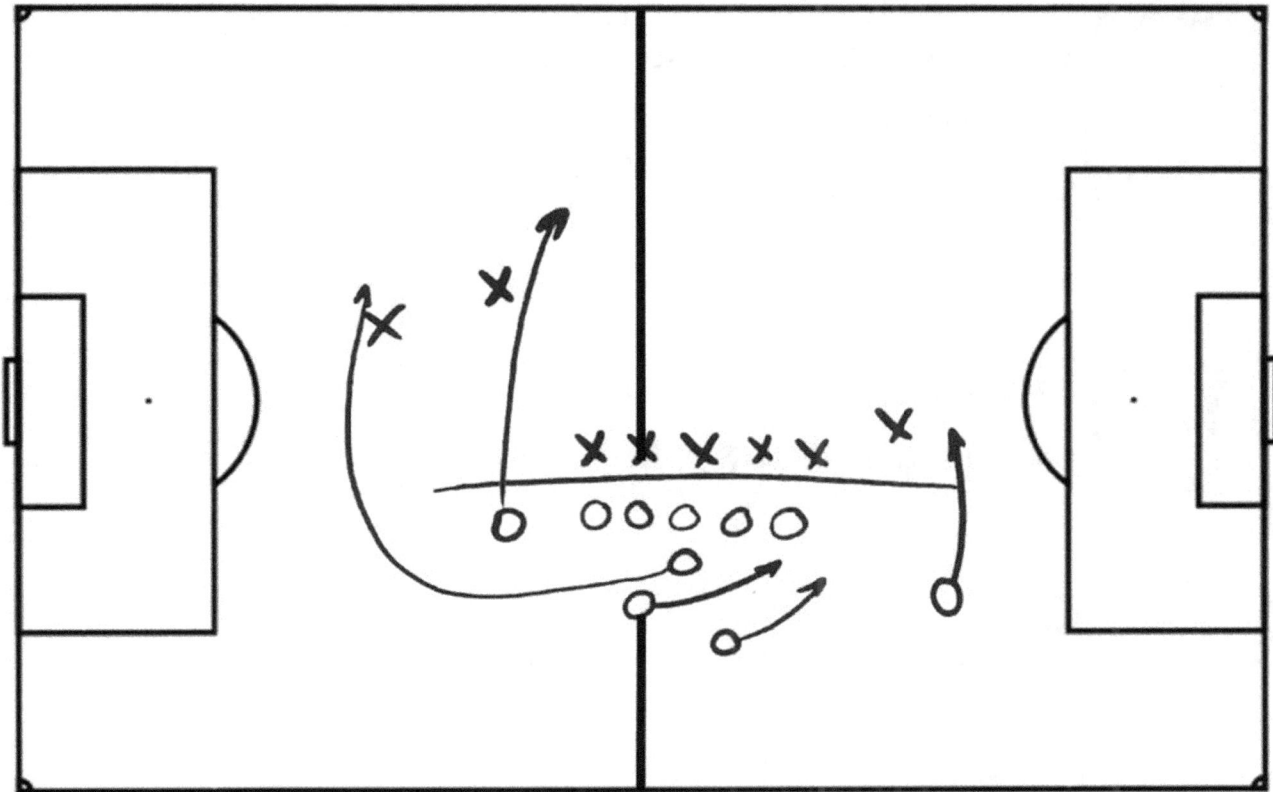

NOTHING NEW

Ecclesiastes – God's Game Plan

Day 1

The Locker Room

You will need:

☐ Ecclesiastes Chapter Three (see Appendix A)

☐ Vanity Chart (Appendix B)

☐ Under the Sun Chart (Appendix C)

☐ Cross Reference Scriptures (Appendix E)

Warm up

- What techniques do you use to manage your time?

- What would be different in your life if you had no fear of the Lord?

- Why do you think there is so much dissatisfaction in people today?

o Read through Ecclesiastes 3. Mark references to time *(include words for forever and eternity)*. You can use a small green clock as your marking. Also, mark all references to God. Make sure you mark any other words from your bookmark. This may take several readings to accomplish all the markings, and it will help you internalize the text even more.

First Quarter

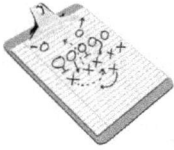

Day 2

Sideline: Ecclesiastes 3:1-11

- What does The Teacher say about time? (3:1; 11)

Summarize the "time" verses by using a chart to make two groups of thoughts. I've filled in the first two. You finish the rest. What pattern do you see?

A Time for Every Event Under Heaven	
To give birth	To die
To plant	To uproot

- Why is man concerned about eternity? (3:11)

Ecclesiastes – God's Game Plan

- Why do you think God placed the desire for man to know about eternity?

    - What does The Teacher say man will not find out? (3:11)

Eternity H 5796 - o-lawm'-
1) long duration, antiquity, futurity, for ever, ever, everlasting, evermore, perpetual, old, ancient, world
a) ancient time, long time (of past)
b) (of future)
1) forever, always
2) continuous existence, perpetual
3) everlasting, indefinite, or unending future, eternity

Run the Play: Application

- How does understanding God's timing affect our ability to:

    - Manage our time wisely?

    - Recognize and respond to opportunities?

    - Examine our relationships?

- Read the following verses (See Appendix E) How would you respond to the Teacher about man's inability to search out the works of God (3:11)

    - Pr. 25:2

    - Mark 4:10-13

    - 1 Cor. 2:6-16

- How would you tell someone how having a relationship with Jesus can change one's perspective on life?

Day 3

Second Quarter- Ecclesiastes 3:12-22

Sideline - *(Remember, the sideline is where you observe the text and get the interpretation to run the play)*

- According to the author, what is a gift from God? (3:12-13)

- What does Solomon say about the things that God does? (3:14)

    o How are we to respond to that knowledge? (3:14)

- What does God seek? (3:15)

    o How does verse 3:15 represent the unchanging nature of God?

- How can you use past "patterns" to gain insight into the present and the future? (3:15)

- What did Solomon see and understand about the wicked and the righteous? (3:16-17)

- Why does God test us? (3:18)

Finish the patterns:

1,1, 2,2 ,3,3,
4.........................0,0

AZ, BY, CX,
DW...........................
....

☆ ♡ △ ......
☆ ♡ △

How can you determine
what is next?

Ecclesiastes – God's Game Plan

- With what does He test us? (Keep in context of preceding verses).

- How did Solomon compare men to beasts? (3:18-21)

Run the Play: Application

- How can we be hopeful and see good in our labor (work, occupation, vocation, ministry, etc.)?

  - Give examples of how living without the fear of the Lord is seen today?

- How do you come to terms or have peace with seeing wickedness and injustice seemingly prevail?

- Read the following verses and explain how we can have peace amid a wicked and evil generation. (see Appendix E).

  - Romans 14:10-15

  - I Corinthians 4:5

  - Matthew 8:29

- In verse 3:18, Solomon compares men to beasts. Using the Venn Diagram, compare and contrast some characteristics of the wicked and beast. Think beyond physical traits. In what way do you agree or disagree with Solomon?

How are they similar? (put similarities in overlapping section)

How are they different? (put differences in outer sections)

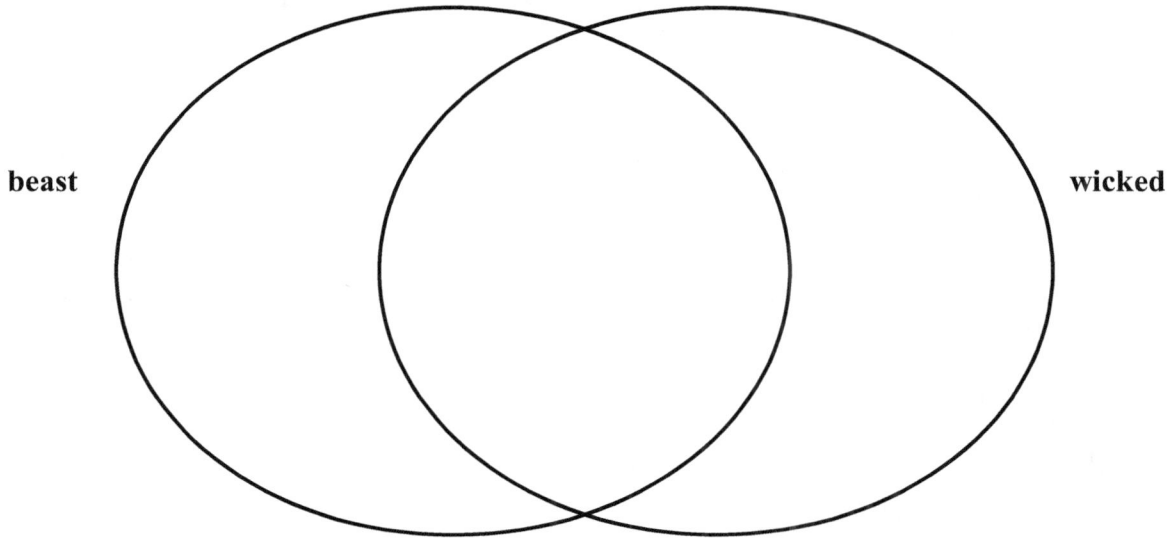

beast   wicked

- What conclusion can you draw about the comparison between the wicked and beast?

Replay: (memory verse)

Take time to ponder God's purpose in timing. Remember that everything has a beginning and an end. What things do you need to begin? What do you need to finish?

31

Day 4

Third Quarter

The Locker Room

You will need:

☐ Ecclesiastes Chapter Four (see Appendix A)

☐ Vanity Chart (Appendix B)

☐ Under the Sun Chart (Appendix C)

☐ Cross Reference Scriptures (see Appendix F)

Warm up

• What is your motivation for success?

• What qualities do you look for in a friend?

Read Ecclesiastes 4. Remember to make your markings. Make sure to mark the words *labor/work* and fill out your "vanity" and "under the sun" charts.

**The Comforter
G3875 - paraklētos**

1) summoned, called to one's side, esp. called to one's aid

a) one who pleads another's cause before a judge, a pleader, counsel for defense, legal assistant, an advocate

b) one who pleads another's cause with one, an intercessor

1) of Christ in his exaltation at God's right hand, pleading with God the Father for the pardon of our sins

c) in the widest sense, a helper, succorer, aider, assistant

1) of the Holy Spirit destined to take the place of Christ with the apostles (after his ascension to the Father), to lead them to a deeper knowledge of the gospel truth, and give them divine strength needed to enable them to undergo trials and

---

Day 5

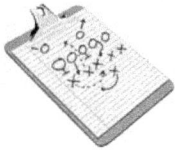

Sideline

- What did Solomon see taking place under the sun? (4:1)

• What did Solomon say about the oppressed and their oppressors? (4:1-3)

    o   In what ways do you see the same oppression and hopelessness in society today?

  o Read the scriptures below (see Appendix F). What would you say to the oppressed to give them hope? *(I know I keep asking that question. Each time you should have more words of wisdom and comfort to share with those looking for hope in their life.)*

      ☐ John 14: 16, 26

      ☐ John 15:26

      ☐ John 16:7-8

• How did Solomon compare the living, the dead, and the unborn? (4:2-3)

    o   In what ways do you agree or disagree with Solomon's assessment?

Ecclesiastes – God's Game Plan

- What did Solomon say was man's motivation for working? (4:4)

  - Why is envy not a good motivation for success?

- What statement did he make about the lazy person and the person who works with the wrong motivation? (4:5-6)

  - What role does contentment play in achieving success?

  - What is the balance between laziness and being a "workaholic"?

- What other vanity did Solomon describe? (4:7-8)

  - What do you think should be the purpose of work and success?

Workaholic

someone who has a compulsive need to work hard and for very long hours

Run the Play: Life Application

- In what ways do you feel your daily tasks are meaningful? What tasks do you find meaningless?

- If success is meaningless, why do people work so hard to achieve it?

- When has envy ever played a role in your desire for advancement?

   - What are some excellent motivators for success?

   - What are some steps you can take to deal with the envy of other's achievements or skills?

- In terms of your work style, rate yourself:

Lazy ⬅━━━━━━━━━━━━━━━━━━━━━➤Workaholic

- What changes do you need to make in your attitude or actions to experience the results of verse 4:6?

Ecclesiastes – God's Game Plan

Day 6

Fourth Quarter

Sideline

- Why does Solomon say partnership is important? (4:9-12)

  ○ Read Proverbs 17:17; 18:24 (see Appendix F). How do they relate to what Solomon says about friendship in Ecclesiastes 4:9-12?

  ○ Why is fellowship with other believers vital?

- What comparison did Solomon make about the wise and the foolish? (4:13-16)

- What final comment does he make about the value of promotion? (4:13-16)

> ### Create Your
> ### "Three-Strand Cord"
>
> ☐ *A person to walk in front of you to lead the way and call you forward*
>
> ☐ *A person to walk beside you to keep you encouraged*
>
> ☐ *A person to walk behind you to keep you from turning back in tough times.*

Run the Play: Application

- Regarding friendship, do you see yourself as dependent or independent of connecting with others?

- Are there any changes you need to make in the way you see friendship and fellowship with others?

- What are some reasons you choose certain partnerships?

- Why is it important to remain teachable?

- How concerned are you about your "likability" factor when aiming for advancement? How much weight should that carry in your goals to succeed? (Reread 4:13-16).

Replay: *(you should recognize the replay button means to choose a verse to commit to memory or a nugget to help you remember what you have learned.)*

Game Highlights: *What motivated you the most this week?*

WEEK THREE

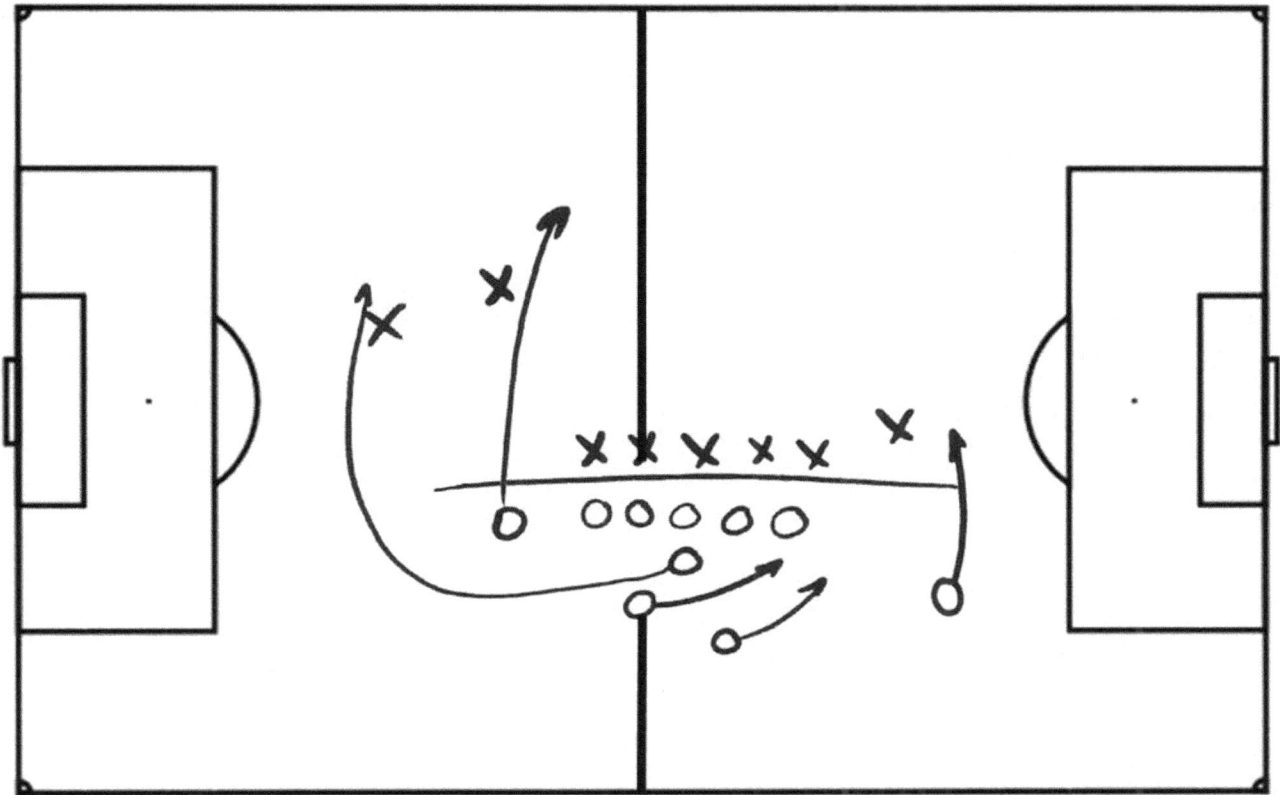

THE PASSION FACTOR

Ecclesiastes – God's Game Plan

Day 1

The Locker Room

You will need:

- ☐ Ecclesiastes Chapter 5 (see Appendix A)
- ☐ Vanity Chart (Appendix B)
- ☐ Under the Sun Chart (Appendix C)
- ☐ Cross Reference Scriptures (see Appendix G)

Warm up

- Have you ever made promises that you didn't/couldn't keep? How did you feel after breaking your promise? How did the person feel?

- How satisfied are you with your life in general (family, work, purpose, health, etc.)?

⟵─────────────────────────────⟶

Not very satisfied   somewhat satisfied   satisfied

- In what specific areas of your life would you like to see improvement in regards to satisfaction?

Read Ecclesiastes 5. Mark your keywords and fill out your *"vanity"* and *"under the sun/heaven"* chart. Remember, *"futility, emptiness,* and *striving for the wind"* are the same as vanity.

Day 2

First Quarter – Ecclesiastes 5:1-9

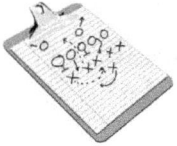

Sideline: *(remember, the sideline is the place to observe and get instruction before running the play.)*

- How should a person go to the house of God? (5:1)

  - Read Psalm 122:1 (see Appendix G)
    - What should be our attitude?

- What should be our conduct in the house of God (5:1-3)

- What did Solomon say concerning making vows? (5:4-6)

- Read the following verses (see Appendix G)

  ☐ Numbers 30:2

  ☐ Deuteronomy 23:21-23

  ☐ Psalm 66:13- 14

  ☐ Proverbs 20:25

  ☐ Matthew 5:33-35

The Definition of a Vow

Simply viewed, offering a vow is practicing a kind of "credit card" act of worship. It is a promise to worship God with a certain offering in the future, motivated by gratitude for God's grace in the life of the offerer. The reason for the delay in making the offering was that the offerer was not able, at that moment to make the offering. The vow was made, promising to offer something to God if God would intervene on behalf of the individual, making the offering possible. In many instances, the vow was made in a time of great danger or need. The Rabbis believed that the gifts which were vowed in Leviticus 27 were to be used for the maintenance of the Temple.

- *Keil and Delitzsch* define the term vow in this way: "… a vow was a promise made by anyone to dedicate and give his own person, or a portion of his property, to the Lord for averting some danger and distress, or for bringing to his possession some desired earthly good.—Besides ordinary vowing or promising to give, there was also vowing away, or the vow of renunciation of something {such as the vow of a Nazarite.}

- How important are vows made to God?

- What does Solomon say we should do to avoid being hasty with our mouths? (5:7)

- What shouldn't we be shocked at seeing? Why? (5:8-9)

Run the Play

o How do you prepare yourself to come into the House of the Lord?

- Why is the right attitude about approaching God in worship crucial?

- What can cause you to have an improper attitude when coming to the house of the Lord?

Standing in awe of God...

A mixture of wonder and dread;

a feeling of amazement and respect mixed with fear that is often coupled with a feeling of personal insignificance or powerlessness.

God is awesome because...

1.

2.

3.

4.

5.

6.

7.

8.

9.

10.

- What causes people to make hasty promises to God? Give some examples.

- What vows have you made to God that you need to fulfill?

- What about God causes you to be in awe of Him? Take a moment to list these things and use them in your prayer time to remind yourself and God how great He is.

- Why is corruption in government, business, ministry, etc., so rampant?

o How has this corruption affected the trust of the people they serve?

o What can you do to hold leaders accountable?

Ecclesiastes – God's Game Plan

Day 3

Second Quarter- Ecclesiastes 5:10-20

Sideline

- What does Solomon say about those who love money? (5:10)

- What did Solomon say were some disadvantages of increased wealth? (5:11-12)

  - How can increased wealth cause sleeplessness?

- Why is focusing on and hoarding money not beneficial to us? (5:13-17)

- What health-related issues can result from "the love of money"? (5:17)

Did you know….

According to experts being a millionaire is "a surefire recipe for unhappiness." It's even got a name: *Wealthy Fatigue Syndrome.* Apparently more and more rich people are coming down with this issue, which means they're finding it harder and harder to stay interested in life and end up taking more and more risks both financially and physically to make things exciting -- much like an addiction. The cure? It depends on the person really, but in most cases getting back to the small simple pleasures in life, and not worrying about always having the biggest and the best of everything, is key.

http://www.thatsfit.com

Do not wear yourself out to get rich; do not trust your own cleverness. Proverbs 23:4

● What is the gift that God has given men concerning wealth? (5:18-20)

Run the Play:

Read the following verses (Appendix G)

☐ Job 1:21

☐ Matthew 6:19-21,24

☐ I Timothy 6:6-10

☐ Hebrews 13:56

● How do you balance being content with your desire to progress?

● Since we know we don't take anything with us when we die, what is the point of acquiring wealth?

● What are your desires/purpose regarding acquiring wealth?

- What do you need to change about your thinking or actions to reflect the right attitude about acquiring wealth? Are there any changes you need to make in your priorities?

 Replay:

Take a moment to ponder the purpose of wealth. Do a little research to see what percentage of lottery winners go broke in a few years. How important do you think your purpose is to your wealth accumulation? "

The Locker Room

Day 4

You will need:

☐ Ecclesiastes Chapter 6 (see Appendix A)

☐ Vanity Chart (Appendix B)

☐ Under the Sun Chart (Appendix C)

☐ Cross Reference Scriptures (see Appendix H)

Warm up

● What do you find most enjoyable about your life?

● Describe what your life would look like if all your desires were fulfilled.

Read Ecclesiastes 6. Take time to make your markings and fill out your charts. Take a moment to review your charts. Any thoughts about what you see so far? That's all for today.

Ecclesiastes – God's Game Plan

Day 5

Third Quarter- Ecclesiastes 6:1-6

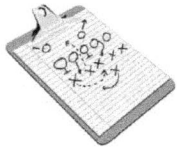

Sideline

- What evil did Solomon notice? (6:1-2)

    o What would prevent someone from enjoying what they have worked hard to obtain?

    o How would a "foreigner" be able to enjoy the benefits?

    o Give a modern-day example of this happening.

- Why did Solomon say a miscarriage was better than life sometimes? (6:3-5)

    o What circumstances might cause a person to want death instead of life?

- What common thing does the stillborn and the living share? (6:6)

Run the Play

- What are some changes you can make to ensure that you are enjoying life more?

- What would you say to someone who commonly forgoes pleasurable pursuits (family time, hobbies, vacation, worship, etc.) to accumulate wealth?

Ecclesiastes – God's Game Plan

Day 6

Fourth Quarter- Ecclesiastes 6:7-12

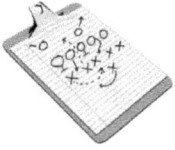

Sideline

- What observation did Solomon make about work and our appetite? (6:7)

  ○ How can our appetites be difficult to satisfy?

  ○ What kind of appetite do you think he is referring to in this passage?

- What was his question about the wise man and the fool? (6:8)

  ○ In what way could a wise person be no better off than a fool?

- What advice did Solomon give about our desires? (6:9)

- How does the following proverb relate to Solomon's statement, *"A bird in the hand is worth two in the bush"*?

- What is his conclusion about life? (6:10-12)

- What are your thoughts on "wishful thinking"?

- Look at the following verses (see Appendix H). How do they relate to 6:10?

    ○ Psalm 139:16

    ○ Proverbs 20:24

    ○ Romans 8:28-30

- Read the following. Tie in the saying "life is short" with Solomon's final thoughts.

    ○ Psalm 39:5

    ○ Psalm 144:3-4

    ○ James 4:14

- How does the cliché "talk is cheap" compare to what Solomon said about our words? Can you give some examples?

Ecclesiastes – God's Game Plan

 **Run the Play**

- How often do you dream and talk about your goals more than you work to pursue them?

- What practical steps can you take to make those goals a reality?

- Describe your satisfaction once you accomplish your goals.

- Who will benefit from your accomplishments?

My dream is . . . .

 Replay:

 **Game Highlights:** *My Prayer....*

WEEK FOUR

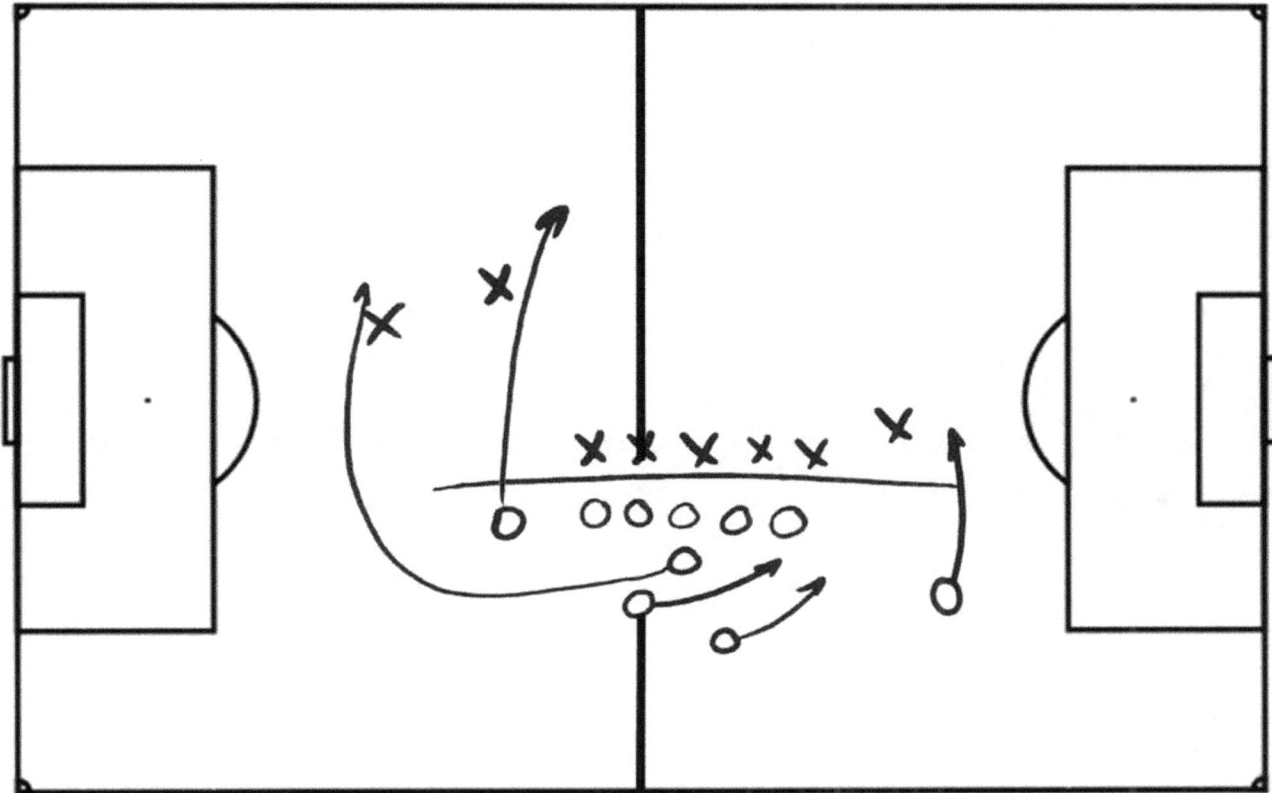

WHEN WISDOM RULES

Ecclesiastes – God's Game Plan

Day 1

Chapter 6 asked, "Who knows what is good?" Chapter 7 gives some answers.

The Locker Room

- ☐ You will need:
- ☐ Ecclesiastes Chapter 7 (see Appendix A)
- ☐ Vanity Chart (Appendix B)
- ☐ Under the Sun Chart (Appendix C)
- ☐ Cross Reference Scriptures (see Appendix I)

Warm up

- If you could choose to go only to funerals or go to parties for the next 12 months, which one would you choose? Why?

- Describe a time when you were discontented with God when He didn't intervene on your behalf to change a situation?

- What moment in your past would you like to relive? What would you want to change about this moment if you could (decisions, actions, words…)? *Bonus: Write a short note to your past self about that time (advice, encouragement, warning….).*

- Read Chapter 7 and make your markings. Fill out your vanity and under the sun charts.

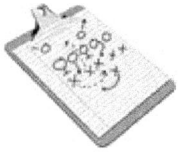

Day 2

First Quarter-- Ecclesiastes 7:1-14

Sideline: Why is it better to go to the house of mourning than to the house of feasting? (7:1-2)

- Why is sorrow better than laughter? (7:3)

    o How can a person have a sad face have a happy heart?

- Where can you find the mind of the wise? (7:4)

    o Why would a wise person prefer the house of mourning?

- How can a rebuke from a wise person be better than praise from a fool? (7:5-6)

Crackling Thorns

Thorns were a rapidly burning, easily extinguishable fuel in the ancient world." (Eaton)

"They make a great noise, a great blaze; and are extinguished in a few moments. Such indeed, comparatively, are the joys of life; they are noisy, flashy, and transitory." (Clarke)

The laughter of a fool is, which may fitly be compared to the burning of thorns under a pot, which makes a great noise and a great blaze, for a little while, but is gone presently, scatters its ashes, and contributes scarcely any thing to the production of a boiling heat, for that requires a constant fire! The laughter of a fool is noisy and flashy and is not an instance of true joy. This is also vanity; it deceives men to their destruction, for the end of that mirth is heaviness…

Ecclesiastes – God's Game Plan

- Read the following verses (Appendix I) and discuss how oppression (extortion) and bribery can affect the wise? (7:7)

    - ☐ Exodus 23:8

    - ☐ Matthew 28:12-15

    - ☐ Mark 11:9-11

    - ☐ Luke3:13

- How should we respond to the temptation to extort or accept bribes? Why?

    - ☐ Proverbs 15:26-27

    - ☐ Psalm 15

- Why should we be slow to anger? (7:9)

    - ☐ Proverbs 29:11

    - ☐ Proverbs 16:32

    - ☐ James 1:19-20

- Why should we avoid longing for things of the past? (7:10)

- What advantage does wisdom have over money? (7:11-12)

Look at this picture. Describe what you see?

- How should we respond to prosperity and adversity? (7:13-14)

  o I Samuel 2:7-8

  o Job 2:10

  o Ecclesiastes 3:22

  o James 1:2-4

- What are some adverse effects of longing for the past?

Run the Play:

- Would you rather spend a week being critiqued or praised? How do you think you feel at the end of the week? Why?

- Appoint some "wise men" in these areas of your life and submit yourself to listen to wisdom.

  o Spiritual life

  o Family life (marriage, parenting, …)

  o Business and finance

Ecclesiastes – God's Game Plan

- o   Health

- o   Other

- How do you typically respond to adversity? What changes do you need to make in your response?

- When do you find yourself "longing" for the past? What can you do to stay present in the moment that you are in right now?

Day 3

Second Quarter – Ecclesiastes 7:15-29

Sideline

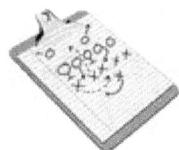

- What did Solomon have to say about the righteous and the wicked? (7:15, 20)

- What was his advice on excessive living? (7:16-18)

☐ In what ways can this kind of excess do more harm than good?

- How does the fear of the Lord benefit us? (7:18)

☐ Read Proverbs 1:7 (Appendix I)

- What is the benefit of godly wisdom? (7:19)

- How should we respond when people speak against us? Why? (7:21-22)

- What did Solomon set out to discover next? (7:23-25)

- What kind of woman is worse than death? (7:26)

☐ Proverbs 2:10-11, 16-18

☐ Proverbs 5:45

Ecclesiastes – God's Game Plan

- How can one escape this kind of woman? (7:26)

- What did Solomon find while he was still searching? (7:27-28)

- How did God originally design mankind? What has changed His design? (7:29)

    ☐ Genesis 1:26-27

    ☐ Genesis 6:5-6

    ☐ I Corinthians 5:1-2

Run the Play

- Why do some people live life to the extreme when it comes to sin or holiness?

- What kind of extremes have you noticed in society today?

- In what areas of your own life do you need to be careful about going to the extreme?

- How do you react when you know someone has been speaking negatively about you? Why do you have this response?

- How much effort do you make to avoid speaking negatively about others?

- What kind of wicked "devices" do you see that man has created today? What are the consequences?

 **Replay:**

Day 4

Locker Room Chapter 8 (side box-Oaths)

You will need:

☐ Ecclesiastes Chapter 8 (see Appendix A)

☐ Vanity Chart (Appendix B)

☐ Under the Sun Chart (Appendix C)

☐ Cross Reference Scriptures (see Appendix J)

Warm up

- When have you questioned the wisdom or actions of those in leadership?

- How did you respond to frustration with those in leadership positions?

Read Chapter 8 and make your markings. Fill out your vanity and under the sun charts.

Day 5

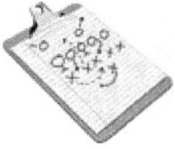

Third Quarter- Ecclesiastes 8:1-9

Sideline:

- What does wisdom do for us? (8:1)

- How are we to respond to authority? (8:2-3)

- Why are oaths important?

- What types of authority are we to obey today?

  - How are we to address grievances with those in authority? (8:4-6). Read (Appendix J)

    ○ 2 Samuel 12:1-9, 13

    ○ I Timothy 5:19

- What does Solomon say about the future and death? (8:7-8)

- How much authority do we have over the timing of life and death?

Making Oaths

Oaths were commonly ones of allegiance to something or a covenant to someone. They were often legally and morally binding. Oaths were not to be taken lightly (similar to a vow).

People would make oaths of allegiance to kings.

David and Jonathan made covenantal oath in I Samuel 20:14-17. David fulfilled his promise to Jonathan in II Samuel 9:5-6. *Take a few moments to read about them.*

God made an oath not to destroy the world again by water in Genesis 8:20-22.

Many people are required to make oaths:

Doctors

Military Members

President

Bride/Groom

Citizens

Can you think of others?

Ecclesiastes – God's Game Plan

- When is authority a bad thing? (8:9)

Run the Play

- Do you follow all or just some traffic laws (speed, lane changes, not turning on red…)? Why or why not?

o How do you react when others follow the posted speed limit and traffic laws?

o How does your willingness to obey earthly laws reflect on your willingness to obey heavenly commands?

Take the Challenge

Choose at least one day between now and next week to "drive biblically". That means you will follow **ALL** posted traffic signs (speed limits, no turn on red, no passing zones, etc…). Pay attention to how others respond to your obedience. Note any difficulties you encounter when doing this.

Imagine how Jesus felt when those around Him were bothered by His obedience…

- What are some things you can do to ensure our leaders (government, church, work…) act fairly and justly?

How would you handle faulty leadership in the following places:

- o   Church

- o   Work

- o   Government

- o   Home

- o   Other areas?

> ### *How to Honor the Wicked in Death?*
>
> *Obituary for an Abusive Mother*
>
> Marianne Theresa Johnson-Reddick born Jan 4, 1935 and died alone on Aug. 30, 2013.
>
> She is survived by her 6 of 8 children whom she spent her lifetime torturing in every way possible. While she neglected and abused her small children, she refused to allow anyone else to care or show compassion towards them. When they became adults she stalked and tortured anyone they dared to love. Everyone she met, adult or child was tortured by her cruelty and exposure to violence, criminal activity, vulgarity, and hatred of the gentle or kind human spirit.
>
> On behalf of her children whom she so abrasively exposed to her evil and violent life, we celebrate her passing from this earth and hope she lives in the after-life reliving each gesture of violence, cruelty, and shame that she delivered on her children. Her surviving children will now live the rest of their lives with the peace of knowing their nightmare finally has some form of closure.
>
> Most of us have found peace in helping those who have been exposed to child abuse and hope this message of her final passing can revive our message that abusing children is unforgivable, shameless, and should not be tolerated in a "humane society". Our greatest wish now, is to stimulate a national movement that mandates a purposeful and dedicated war against child abuse in the United States of America.

- Are there any areas in which you struggle with being in authority and exercising justice and fairness?

- As a leader, what would be your "golden rule" regarding exercising authority?

- How do the following verses give you a different outlook on death than Solomon had?

  ☐ Romans 5:12-17

  ☐ Hebrews 9:27-28

Day 6

Fourth Quarter- Ecclesiastes 8:10-17

Sideline:

- What did Solomon see concerning the wicked? (8:10)

- Why are they (or their deeds) "soon forgotten" in the very place they did wickedness?

- What happens when evil is not dealt with promptly? (8:11)

- How does having or not having the proper attitude toward God affect the righteous and wicked? (8:12-13)

- What does Solomon say about apparent injustice? (8:14)

  - How should we respond to this? (8:15) (Appendix J)

☐ Psalm 37:7

☐ Psalm 73

Ecclesiastes – God's Game Plan

- What did Solomon say it is impossible to discover? (8:16-17)

  - Instead of spending time trying to "figure God out," what should we do?

  ☐ Psalm 40:5

  ☐ John 21:24-25

 **Run the Play**

- Give a modern-day example of the wicked being celebrated in their death (public mourning, lavish funeral, etc.)

  - Why is all the celebration of an unrighteous person meaningless?

- What can you do this week to continue to cultivate a healthy fear of God?

  - Read: Philippians 4:10-13

- Why is it sometimes difficult to find contentment in adversity?

- In what areas of your life do you need to practice being joyful and content? How will you do this?

    O Church

    O Work

    O Government

    O Home

    O Other

Replay

Game Highlights: Prayer

WEEK FIVE

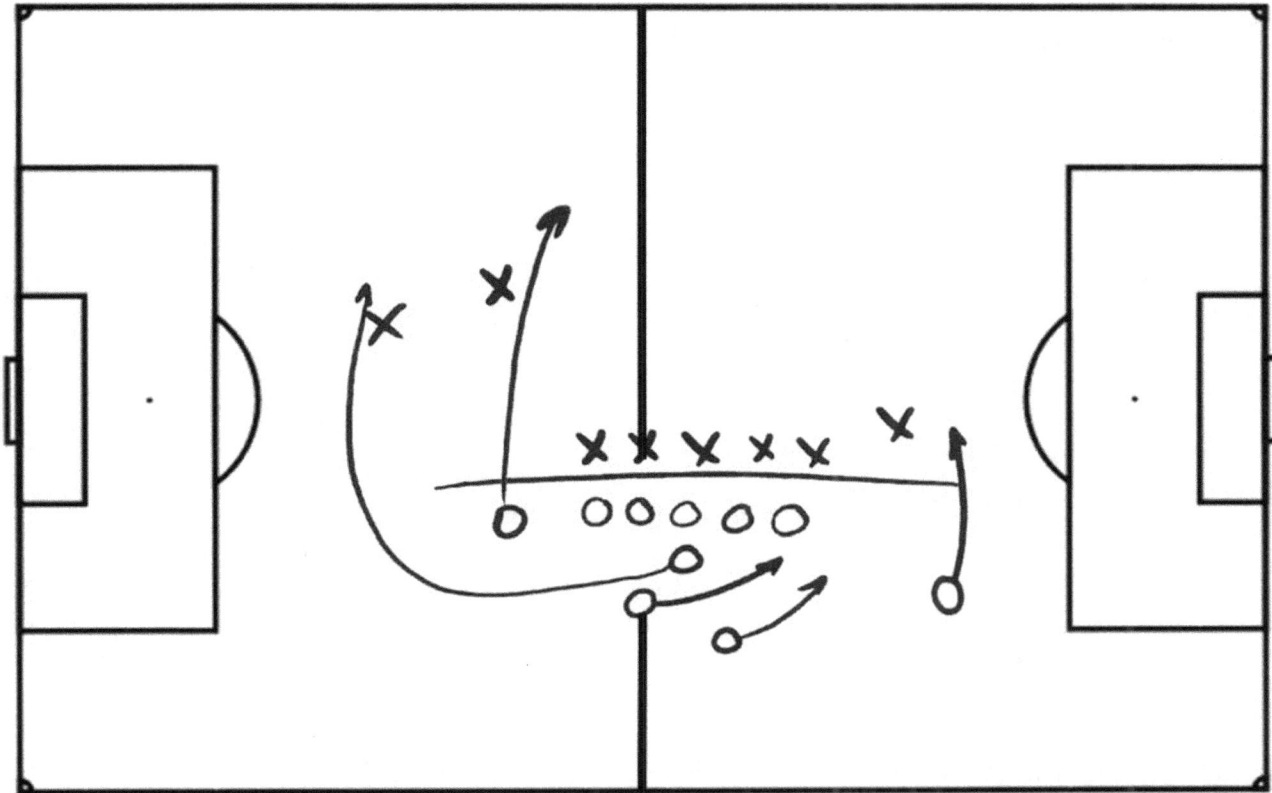

THE POWER OF WISDOM

Ecclesiastes – God's Game Plan

Day 1

The Locker Room

☐ Ecclesiastes Chapter 9 (see Appendix A)

☐ Vanity Chart (Appendix B)

☐ Under the Sun Chart (Appendix C)

☐ Cross Reference Scriptures (see Appendix K)

Warm up

• Would you want to know when/how you were going to die? Why or why not?

• What would you do if you knew you only had six months to live?

• Which would you rather possess in abundance, wisdom or wealth? Why?

Read Chapter 9 and make your markings. Fill out your vanity and under the sun charts.

Day 2

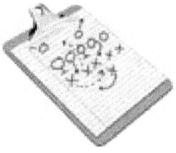

First Quarter- Ecclesiastes 9:1-10

Sideline

- What did Solomon want to explain to people about life and death? (9:1-3)

- Why are men's hearts full of evil? (9:3)

Read the following passages (Appendix K):

- ☐ I Corinthians 6:9-11
- ☐ Galatians 5:19-21
- ☐ Ephesians 5:5
- ☐ Galatians 6:7-8

  ○ What's the point of living righteously if everyone dies anyway?

- In chapter 4, Solomon declared that the dead or unborn had it better than the living. What advantage does he now say the living have over the dead? (9:4-6)

- In light of the inevitability of death, what is Solomon's advice? (9:7)

Ecclesiastes – God's Game Plan

- What kind of attitude are we to have about life and work? (9:8,10)

    o Proverbs 22:29

    o I Corinthians 15:57-58

    o Colossians 3:23-25

- What reward has God given us? (9:9)

 **Run the Play**

- Solomon presents a very bleak outlook on life and death. How does your knowledge of Jesus Christ give you a different perspective on life and death?

- How does hopelessness in life and death spur evil in society?

- How do you typically approach unwanted or disliked tasks?

- What changes do you need to make in your attitude about these tasks?

Day 3

Second Quarter - Ecclesiastes 9:11-18

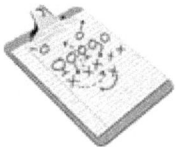

Sideline

- What is a common denominator among all people? (9:11)

- What happens to fish caught in nets? (Imagine you are a fish, tell your story from a fish's viewpoint)

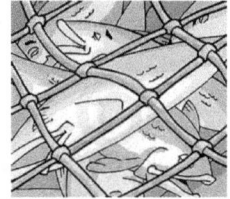

    o How does this compare with the timing of one's death? (9:12)

- Solomon told a story about a poor but wise man who saved a city. What was the point of this story? (9:13-17)

    o Why do you think a poor person is despised and often ignored? Is this fair?

        o Read Proverbs 14:20; Proverbs 19:7; James 2:6 (Appendix K)

- What can cause damage to what wisdom has built? (9:18)

Run the Play

- How should knowing the certainty of death yet the uncertainty of time change your outlook on life?

    o Read Ephesians 5:15-17

Ecclesiastes – God's Game Plan

- Do you have a "Bucket List" *(a list of things you want to experience/accomplish before you die)*? What steps have you taken to accomplish those things? If you don't have one started, get a sheet of paper and create one. Watch the movie "The Bucket List" to get a few ideas if you need help.

- When have you been tempted to show partiality based on wealth (or lack of) or status?

- How does this reflect the character of God?

  Romans 2:10-11

- How can wrong associations destroy good works? Read the following (Appendix K)

  - Joshua 7:1,5,7, 10-12, 20-21,25 (the story of Achan)

  - I Kings 11:4

  - I Corinthians 11:4

- What relationship do you need to reevaluate in your life?

 **Replay:**

Day 4

Locker Room

You will need:

☐ Ecclesiastes Chapter 10 (see Appendix A)

☐ Vanity Chart (Appendix B)

☐ Under the Sun Chart (Appendix C)

☐ Cross Reference Scriptures (see Appendix L)

Warm up

● How did your driving challenge go this week? What was difficult obeying the limits? How did people respond to you?

● How can you identify visitors to a city/country?

● What are the most dangerous characteristics of snakes?

Read Chapter 10 and make your markings. Fill out your vanity and under the sun charts.

Day 5

Third Quarter Ecclesiastes 10:1-11

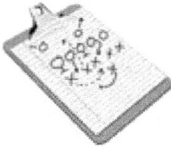

Sideline:

- How does Ecclesiastes 10:1 relate to Ecclesiastes 9:18?

- How can a "little" bit of some things be destructive? (10:1)

Read: (see Appendix L)

- ○ Luke 12:1-3

- ○ I Corinthians 5:6-8

- ○ Proverbs 6:10-11

Do you want to know more about the significance of the right vs. left?

Look up the following passages:

Gen. 48:13-17

Exodus15:6, 12

Psalm 17:7, 18:35

Matthew 26:64

Leviticus 8:23-24

Psalm 16:11

Mark 16:19

Luke 22:69

Acts 2:25

Matt. 25:31-33

- What did Solomon say about the heart of the wise man and the fool? (10:2)

- How does the fool expose himself? (10:3; 15)

- Why should we stay calm in the face of an angry "ruler"? (10:4)

Read the following: Proverbs 25:15

- What evil did he see from those that rule? (10:5-7)

  o Why does he call it an error? Read the following passages.

    ▪ Proverbs 19:10

    ▪ Proverbs 30:21-22

- What are the dangers of not using good judgment and wisdom when attempting to complete a task? (10:8-9)

- What is a necessary ingredient to make success more likely when working on projects? (10:11)

Run the Play

- Are there any "small things" in your life you need to address before they bring ruin to your image or your witness?

  o Ecclesiastes 7:1a

  o Solomon 2:15

- What are your thoughts about seeing seemingly unqualified people in prominent and influential positions? How does it happen? What are the pitfalls?

- Are there any tasks that you need to accomplish that require you to seek wisdom from others? Do you tend to seek help quickly, or are you more hesitant to ask for help?

Day 6

Fourth Quarter- Ecclesiastes 10:11-20

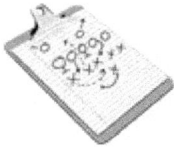

Sideline

• How did Solomon compare a babbler to a serpent? (10:11)

• What are some traits of a serpent/snake that make it dangerous?

• Take a look at the Time Out box on this page. Explain Solomon's comparison of the serpent and the babbler. How can a babbler be "charmed"?

• Continuing with his thoughts on the mouth, what does Solomon say about the fool's mouth compared to the wise man's mouth? Who is harmed by a fool's words? (10:12-14). Read the following (Appendix L)

  ○ Proverbs 10:32

  ○ Proverbs 18:7

• How do the modern-day clichés "Keep it simple stupid" and "Work smarter, not harder" help you understand verse 10:15?

Charming the Serpent

The instrument that is used to mesmerize the snake is a flute made of a wood-like material and a gourd.

It is widely believed that snakes are lulled into a complacent state by the music the snake charmer plays and that they are literally "dancing to the music." This is not actually the case. **Snakes have poor hearing and cannot hear the music.** What is most likely happening is that the snake is reacting to the movements of the flute and slight vibrations in the ground. When the snake rises out of its basket, it is just going into its natural defensive posture.

While training, the flute is often struck by the snake and the snake quickly realizes the pain and fruitless nature of their attacks on the instrument.

The Snakes Mouth…

Anacondas, pythons, and boas grab prey with their teeth, which curve backward, making it nearly impossible for the prey to escape. Then they wrap or constrict around the prey, suffocating or subduing it.

- What does Solomon have to say about immaturity and leadership? (10:16-17)

- How do the conditions of one's area of responsibility reflect their level of maturity and wisdom? (10:18)

  ○ Proverbs 24:30-34

- How can financial planning be an indicator of wisdom? (10:19)

- How does a wise person determine financial priorities? (10:19)

- Do you agree with Solomon on the power of money? What situations can you think of that money may not be the answer?

- What is Solomon's advice about how you talk about people when not in their presence? (10:20)

Run the Play

- What changes can you make in how you handle (charm) babbling fools?

Ecclesiastes – God's Game Plan

- Read the following verses

  ○ Colossians 4:6

  Mark 9:50

  Matthew 5:13

- Rate yourself regarding your words daily.

$$\longleftrightarrow$$

Too Spicy   Salted   Too Sweet

- Ask someone whom you trust to rate you. Is there is a difference? What changes do you need to make to ensure your speech is gracious? How can you model the example of "telling the truth in/with love"?

- In what area of financial management do you need to improve to reflect godly wisdom and maturity?

▶ **Replay:**

Game Highlights: Prayer

WEEK SIX

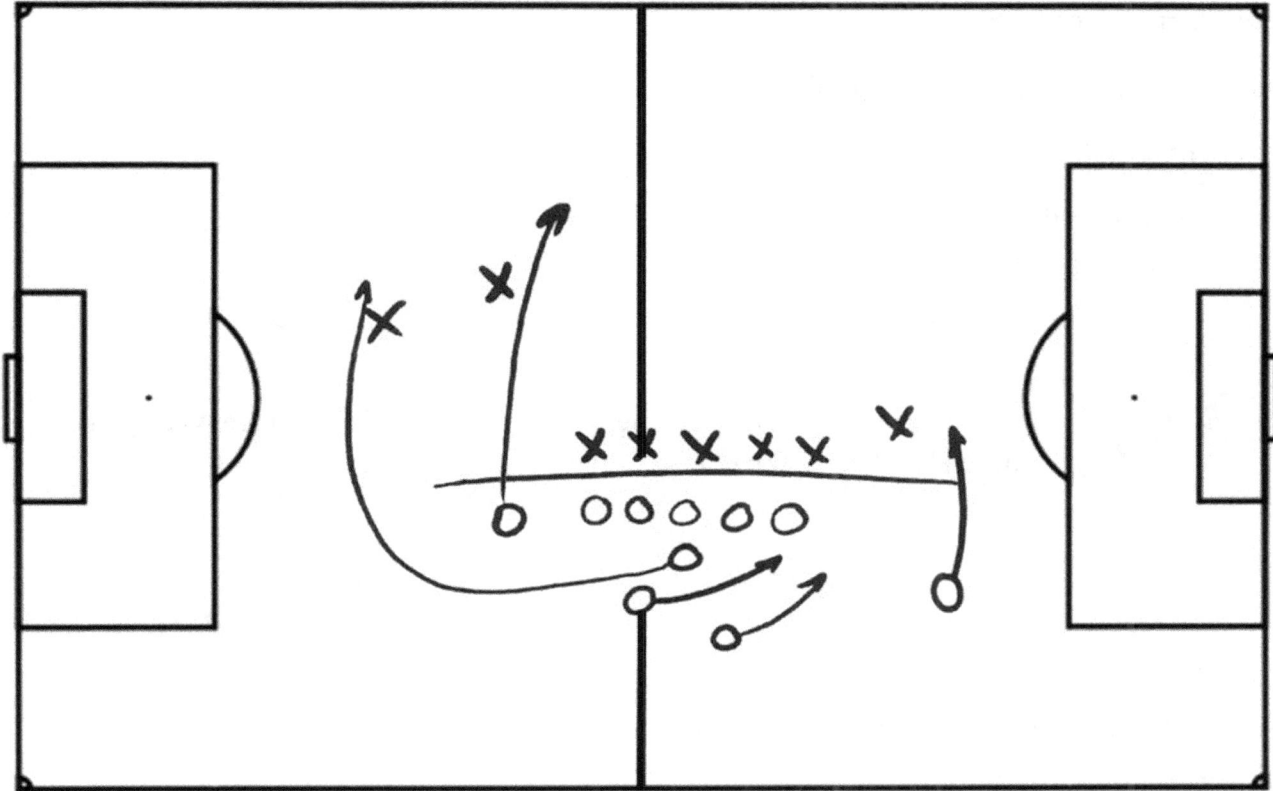

PURPOSE - THERE IS A PLAN

Ecclesiastes – God's Game Plan

Day 1

The Locker Room

You will need:

Ecclesiastes Chapter 11 (Appendix A)

Vanity Chart (Appendix B)

Cross Reference Scriptures (see Appendix M)

Pie Chart (Appendix N)

PICK Chart (Appendix R)

Warm up

- Are you more generous when you have plenty than you are when you don't have abundance? Why?

- How much of a risk-taker are you when it comes to business opportunities? Why?

- Read Chapter 11 and make your markings.

Day 2

First Quarter -Ecclesiastes 11:1-6

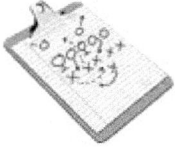

Sideline:

- What did Solomon advise us to do? (11:1-2)

  o What can happen to bread (in some versions, it's called grain) cast upon waters?

- Read the following verses (Appendix M)

  o Deuteronomy 15:10-11

  o Proverbs 19:17

  o Matthew 10:42

  o II Corinthians 9:8-12

- What nugget of advice Solomon is sharing by telling us to cast our bread/grain?

- What benefit may we reap if we "cast our bread"? (11:2)

- What kind of person did Solomon criticize? (11:3-4)

- Why did he criticize this kind of person? (11:5)

Ecclesiastes – God's Game Plan

- What does he say to do in regards to sowing seeds? (11:6)

  - What happens when a farmer doesn't sow seeds or fails to sow seeds at the proper time?

  - How does this relate to us today in terms of opportunities?

Run the Play

- What keeps you from being generous sometimes?

- How important is faith in God's provision for your needs when it comes to sowing (into people, projects, purpose, business…)

  - Use the chart in Appendix N to brainstorm ways to divide your "portions."

PICK ME!!!!!

PICK charts are used in business environments to help groups evaluate, categorize and compare multiple improvement ideas to decide which ideas to implement. Ideas are evaluated according to four characteristics which are represented on the two axes of the chart, creating four quadrants.

The four characteristics are: high payoff, low payoff, hard to do and easy to do.

These create four categories that correspond with the letters of the acronym "PICK":

Possible (low payoff, easy to do), Implement (high payoff, easy to do), Challenge (high payoff, hard to do) and Kill (low payoff, hard to do).

http://www.ehow.com/how

- What types of risks will cause you to hesitate to move forward with an idea or plan?

- What opportunities to bring financial increase have you neglected to take advantage of in the past?

- Is there a "spiritual" risk (leap of faith) that you have avoided?

- What one opportunity or idea keeps tugging at you? What steps do you need to take to seize the moment? *Look at the sample of a PICK Chart (See Appendix R) to assist you in making decisions regarding opportunities. Of course, prayer and allowing Holy Spirit to lead you are the most important decision-making steps.*

Day 3

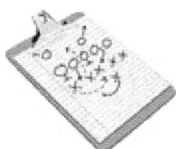

Second Quarter- Ecclesiastes 11:7-10

Sideline

- What is man to do concerning light and darkness? (11:7-8)

- Read the following (Appendix M):

  o Ecclesiastes 9:10

  o Psalm 115:17-18

  o John 9:4

- Why will the days of darkness be more than the days of light? What is the darkness in these verses?

- What advice does Solomon give the young? (11:9-10)

- What sobering truth should govern our lives? (11:9)

Run the Play: Application

- If today was judgment day, and your life was like a gas tank, what would be the reading on your tank regarding fulfilling your purpose? Full, meaning you have yet to begin to fulfill your purpose, or empty, meaning you have done those things you were created and called to do for the Kingdom of Heaven.

Empty   1/4   1/2   3/4   Full

- What can you do to make the most of the life you are living in the following areas? In other words, what can you do to make sure you "die empty"?

  - Spiritual Life

  - Family Life

  - Self (purpose)

  - Other relationships (friends, business, neighbors...)

 Replay: (memory verse)

Ecclesiastes – God's Game Plan

Day 4

Locker Room

☐ Ecclesiastes Chapter 12 (see Appendix A)

☐ Vanity Chart (Appendix B)

☐ Cross Reference Scriptures (Appendix P)

☐ Purpose Discovery Sheets (Appendix O)

Warm Up

● Do you look forward to aging? Why or why not?

● How would knowing your purpose determine your:

○ Path?

○ Passion?

○ Perception?

○ Pursuits?

● Do you think Solomon knew his purpose? Using the Purpose Discovery sheet, help Solomon discover his purpose (See Appendix O).

● Read Chapter 12 and make your markings.

Day 5

Third Quarter

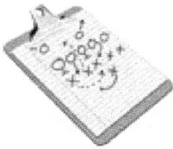

Sideline -Ecclesiastes 12:1-14

- Summarize verses 1-8. When should we remember God? (12:1-7)

- What was Solomon's understanding of the finality of death? (12:8)

- How did Solomon make use of the wisdom he was given? (12:9-10)

Goads

The **goad** is a traditional farming implement, used to spur or guide livestock, usually oxen, which are pulling a plough or a cart; used also to round up cattle. It is a type of a long stick with a pointed end, also known as the cattle prod

- What did he say about the words of the wise and scholars of these collections of words? (12:11)

- Read: (Appendix P)

  o Proverbs 1:1-6

  o Acts 26:13-15

- How can wise words be like goads and scholars like well-placed nails?

- How did he feel about books and studying? (12:12)

Ecclesiastes – God's Game Plan

- Why did he feel this way?

    - I King 4:30-32

    - Ecclesiastes 1:18

- What is his conclusion of the meaning of life? (12:13)

- At the end of the day, how are we all equal to one another? (12:14)

Run the Play

- How can you leave a legacy of wisdom to future generations?

- Since we have no distinction in death, what are you doing in life to cultivate distinction?

Day 6

Fourth Quarter

Sideline: The Conclusion of the Matter

It seems that Solomon spent his life not recognizing the importance of his purpose and how much of an impact his words were making. I don't want you making the same error in your life. You were created on purpose with purpose. You were created to make an impact with your purpose. When you discover YOUR purpose, you will see that life is more than meaningless day-to-day existence. You will walk fulfilled and full of joy and excitement with the light of days you have been gifted. Today is the day for you to begin to *"Make the best use of your time. These are sinful days. Do not be foolish. Understand what the Lord wants you to do."* (Ephesians 5:16-17) Take a look at the charts that you have been completing. If you, like Solomon, feel like what you do is nothing more than "vanity…futile…striving for the wind…emptiness…" then you are not walking in and actively engaged in pursuing your purpose.

Do you know what your purpose is today? If not, let's discover it together. Scan the QR Code or go to www.coachlaurabrown.com and click the schedule/contact button to request a free Purpose Discovery Session. You can also use the Purpose Discovery template in appendix Q.

If you have taken the **Purpose Discovery Course** and still find life unsatisfying, perhaps you need to work on pursuing that purpose. When you walk in your God-given purpose, you will live a productive and fulfilling life, and you will discover your pathways to provision.

Also, realize that you must partner with the ONE who designed you with purpose to fulfill your purpose. We cannot be successful in the Kingdom without a partnership with **THE KING of KINGS**. If you have not entered into a partnership, by accepting Jesus Christ into your heart as your Savior and Lord, now is the day your salvation nearer than before!

"This is what the Scripture says: "The word is near you; it is in your mouth and in your heart." That is the teaching of faith that we are telling. 9 If you declare with your mouth, "Jesus is Lord," and if you believe in your heart that God raised Jesus from the dead, you will be saved. 10 We believe with our hearts, and so we are made right with God. And we declare with our mouths that we believe, and so we are saved. "(Romans 10:8-10)

Solomon had a very bleak outlook on life and death. Although he possessed wisdom, he did not have the full knowledge and understanding of the **Holy One, Jesus Christ of Nazareth!** If you know Jesus as your Savior and Lord, then your hope remains in death even as in life…*" For to this end Christ died and lived again, that He might be Lord both of the dead and of the living." (Romans 14:9)*

You can enjoy life to the fullest, and death will not be something mysterious to be feared or approached with anxiety for *"The Lord will come from heaven with a command, with the voice of the archangel, and with the trumpet call of God. First, the dead who believed in Christ will come back to life. 17 Then, together with them, we who are still alive will be taken in the clouds to meet the Lord in the air. In this way we will always be with the Lord. 18 So then, comfort each other with these words!" (1 Thessalonians 4:16-18)*

So, let us **DIE EMPTY!**

Run the Play: Application

- If you made a confession of your faith today, tell someone. Find a body of believers to connect with so that you may grow in wisdom and knowledge of God and the Kingdom of Heaven.

- Fill out your personal Purpose Discovery Sheet (Appendix Q).

- What steps do you need to take to pursue your purpose?

Replay:

Game Highlights: Prayer

Appendix

Locker Room Equipment

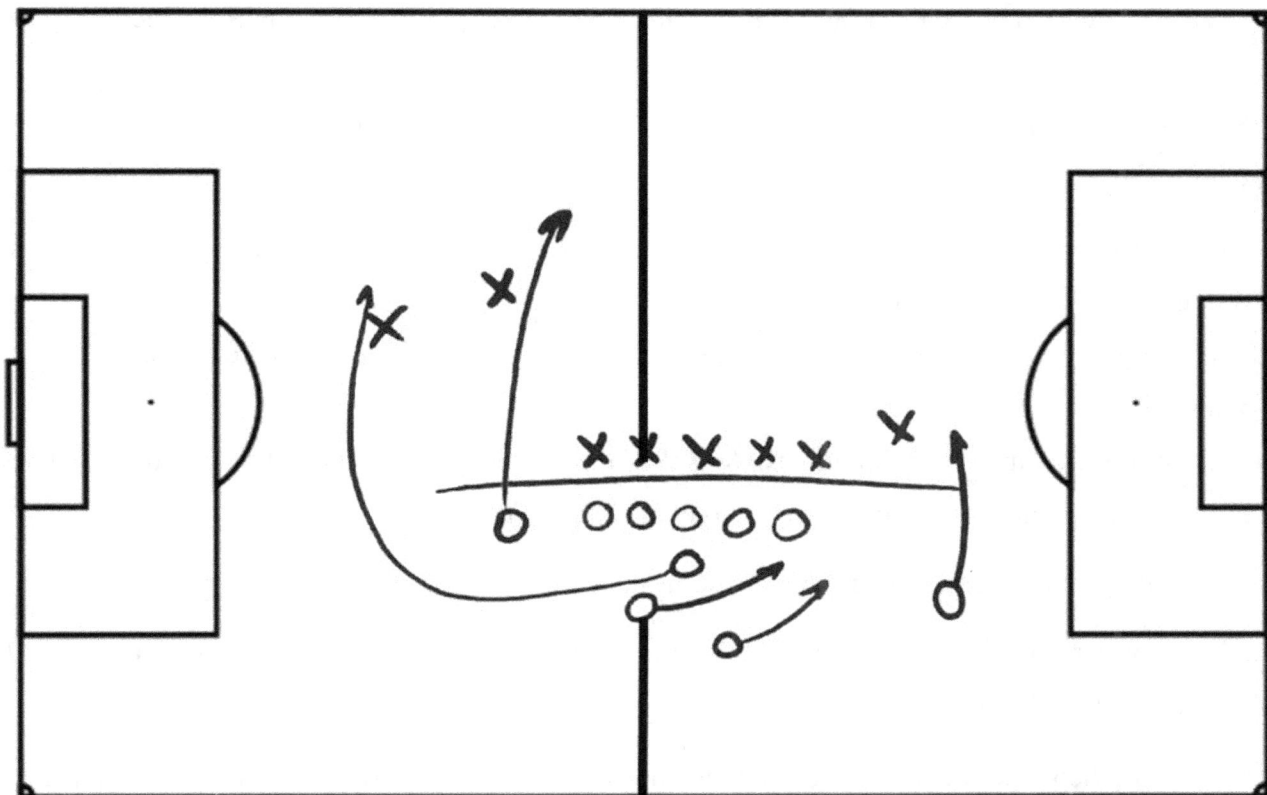

Appendix A

Ecclesiastes 1

1 The words of the Preacher, the son of David, king in Jerusalem.

[2] "Vanity of vanities," says the Preacher, "Vanity of vanities! All is vanity."

[3] What advantage does man have in all his work which he does under the sun?

[4] A generation goes and a generation comes, but the earth remains forever.

[5] Also, the sun rises and the sun sets; and hastening to its place it rises there *again*.

[6] Blowing toward the south, then turning toward the north, the wind continues swirling along; and on its circular courses the wind returns.

[7] All the rivers flow into the sea, yet the sea is not full. To the place where the rivers flow, there they flow again.

[8] All things are wearisome; Man is not able to tell *it*. The eye is not satisfied with seeing, nor is the ear filled with hearing.

[9] That which has been is that which will be, and that which has been done is that which will be done. So there is nothing new under the sun.

[10] Is there anything of which one might say, "See this, it is new"? Already it has existed for ages which were before us.

[11] There is no remembrance of earlier things; And also of the later things which will occur, there will be for them no remembrance among those who will come later *still*.

[12] I, the Preacher, have been king over Israel in Jerusalem.

[13] And I set my mind to seek and explore by wisdom concerning all that has been done under heaven. *It* is a grievous task *which* God has given to the sons of men to be afflicted with.

[14] I have seen all the works which have been done under the sun, and behold, all is vanity and striving after wind.

[15] What is crooked cannot be straightened and what is lacking cannot be counted.

[16] I said to myself, "Behold, I have magnified and increased wisdom more than all who were over Jerusalem before me; and my mind has observed a wealth of wisdom and knowledge."

[17] And I set my mind to know wisdom and to know madness and folly; I realized that this also is striving after wind.

[18] Because in much wisdom there is much grief, and increasing knowledge *results in* increasing pain

Ecclesiastes 2

I said to myself, "Come now, I will test you with pleasure. So enjoy yourself." And behold, it too was futility.

[2] I said of laughter, "It is madness," and of pleasure, "What does it accomplish?"

[3] I explored with my mind *how* to stimulate my body with wine while my mind was guiding *me* wisely, and how to take hold of folly, until I could see what good there is for the sons of men to do under heaven the few years of their lives.

[4] I enlarged my works: I built houses for myself; I planted vineyards for myself;

[5] I made gardens and parks for myself and I planted in them all kinds of fruit trees;

[6] I made ponds of water for myself from which to irrigate a forest of growing trees.

[7] I bought male and female slaves and I had homeborn slaves. Also I possessed flocks and herds larger than all who preceded me in Jerusalem.

[8] Also, I collected for myself silver and gold and the treasure of kings and provinces. I provided for myself male and female singers and the pleasures of men—many concubines.

[9] Then I became great and increased more than all who preceded me in Jerusalem. My wisdom also stood by me.

[10] All that my eyes desired I did not refuse them. I did not withhold my heart from any pleasure, for my heart was pleased because of all my labor and this was my reward for all my labor.

[11] Thus I considered all my activities which my hands had done and the labor which I had exerted, and behold all was vanity and striving after wind and there was no profit under the sun.

[12] So I turned to consider wisdom, madness and folly; for what *will* the man *do* who will come after the king *except* what has already been done?

[13] And I saw that wisdom excels folly as light excels darkness.

[14] The wise man's eyes are in his head, but the fool walks in darkness. And yet I know that one fate befalls them both.

[15] Then I said to myself, "As is the fate of the fool, it will also befall me. Why then have I been extremely

wise?" So I said to myself, ""This too is vanity."

[16] For there is no lasting remembrance of the wise man *as* with the fool, inasmuch as *in* the coming days all will be forgotten. And how the wise man and the fool alike die!

[17] So I hated life, for the work which had been done under the sun was grievous to me; because everything is futility and striving after wind.

[18] Thus I hated all the fruit of my labor for which I had labored under the sun, for I must leave it to the man who will come after me.

[19] And who knows whether he will be a wise man or a fool? Yet he will have control over all the fruit of my labor for which I have labored by acting wisely under the sun. This too is vanity.

[20] Therefore I completely despaired of all the fruit of my labor for which I had labored under the sun.

[21] When there is a man who has labored with wisdom, knowledge and skill, then he gives his legacy to one who has not labored with them. This too is vanity and a great evil.

[22] For what does a man get in all his labor and in his striving with which he labors under the sun?

[23] Because all his days his task is painful and grievous; even at night his mind does not rest. This too is vanity.

[24] There is nothing better for a man *than* to eat and drink and tell himself that his labor is good. This also I have seen that it is from the hand of God.

[25] For who can eat and who can have enjoyment without Him?

[26] For to a person who is good in His sight He has given wisdom and knowledge and joy, while to the sinner He has given the task of gathering and collecting so that he may give to one who is good in God's sight. This too is vanity and striving after wind.

Ecclesiastes 3

There is an appointed time for everything. And there is a time for every event under heaven—

[2] A time to give birth and a time to die; a time to plant and a time to uproot what is planted.

[3] A time to kill and a time to heal; a time to tear down and a time to build up.

[4] A time to weep and a time to laugh; a time to mourn and a time to dance.

[5] A time to throw stones and a time to gather stones; a time to embrace and a time to shun embracing.

[6] A time to search and a time to give up as lost; a time to keep and a time to throw away.

⁷ A time to tear apart and a time to sew together; a time to be silent and a time to speak.

⁸ A time to love and a time to hate; a time for war and a time for peace.

⁹ What profit is there to the worker from that in which he toils?

¹⁰ I have seen the task which God has given the sons of men with which to occupy themselves.

¹¹ He has made everything appropriate in its time. He has also set eternity in their heart, yet so that man will not find out the work which God has done from the beginning even to the end.

¹² I know that there is nothing better for them than to rejoice and to do good in one's lifetime;

¹³ moreover, that every man who eats and drinks sees good in all his labor—it is the gift of God.

¹⁴ I know that everything God does will remain forever; there is nothing to add to it and there is nothing to take from it, for God has *so* worked that men should fear Him.

¹⁵ That which is has been already and that which will be has already been, for God seeks what has passed by.

¹⁶ Furthermore, I have seen under the sun *that* in the place of justice there is wickedness and in the place of righteousness there is wickedness.

¹⁷ I said to myself, "God will judge both the righteous man and the wicked man," for a time for every matter and for every deed is there.

¹⁸ I said to myself concerning the sons of men, "God has surely tested them in order for them to see that they are but beasts."

¹⁹ For the fate of the sons of men and the fate of beasts is the same. As one dies so dies the other; indeed, they all have the same breath and there is no advantage for man over beast, for all is vanity.

²⁰ All go to the same place. All came from the dust and all return to the dust.

²¹ Who knows that the breath of man ascends upward and the breath of the beast descends downward to the earth?

²² I have seen that nothing is better than that man should be happy in his activities, for that is his lot. For who will bring him to see what will occur after him?

Ecclesiastes 4

Then I looked again at all the acts of oppression which were being done under the sun. And behold *I saw* the tears of the oppressed and *that* they had no one to comfort *them*; and on the side of their oppressors was power, but they had no one to comfort *them*.

² So I congratulated the dead who are already dead more than the living who are still living.

³ But better *off* than both of them is the one who has never existed, who has never seen the evil activity that is done under the sun.

⁴ I have seen that every labor and every skill which is done is *the result of* rivalry between a man and his neighbor. This too is vanity and striving after wind.

⁵ The fool folds his hands and consumes his own flesh.

⁶ One hand full of rest is better than two fists full of labor and striving after wind.

⁷ Then I looked again at vanity under the sun.

⁸ There was a certain man without a dependent, having neither a son nor a brother, yet there was no end to all his labor. Indeed, his eyes were not satisfied with riches *and he never asked*, "And for whom am I laboring and depriving myself of pleasure?" This too is vanity and it is a grievous task.

⁹ Two are better than one because they have a good return for their labor.

¹⁰ For if either of them falls, the one will lift up his companion. But woe to the one who falls when there is not another to lift him up.

¹¹ Furthermore, if two lie down together they keep warm, but how can one be warm *alone*?

¹² And if one can overpower him who is alone, two can resist him. A cord of three *strands* is not quickly torn apart.

¹³ A poor yet wise lad is better than an old and foolish king who no longer knows *how* to receive instruction.

¹⁴ For he has come out of prison to become king, even though he was born poor in his kingdom.

¹⁵ I have seen all the living under the sun throng to the side of the second lad who replaces him.

¹⁶ There is no end to all the people, to all who were before them, and even the ones who will come later will not be happy with him, for this too is vanity and striving after wind.

Ecclesiastes 5

Guard your steps as you go to the house of God and draw near to listen rather than to offer the sacrifice of fools; for they do not know they are doing evil.

2 Do not be hasty in word or impulsive in thought to bring up a matter in the presence of God. For God is in heaven and you are on the earth; therefore let your words be few.

3 For the dream comes through much effort and the voice of a fool through many words.

4 When you make a vow to God, do not be late in paying it; for *He takes* no delight in fools. Pay what you vow!

5 It is better that you should not vow than that you should vow and not pay.

6 Do not let your speech cause you to sin and do not say in the presence of the messenger *of God* that it was a mistake. Why should God be angry on account of your voice and destroy the work of your hands?

7 For in many dreams and in many words there is emptiness. Rather, fear God.

8 If you see oppression of the poor and denial of justice and righteousness in the province, do not be shocked at the sight; for one official watches over another official, and there are higher officials over them.

9 After all, a king who cultivates the field is an advantage to the land.

10 He who loves money will not be satisfied with money, nor he who loves abundance *with its* income. This too is vanity.

11 When good things increase, those who consume them increase. So what is the advantage to their owners except to look on?

12 The sleep of the working man is pleasant, whether he eats little or much; but the full stomach of the rich man does not allow him to sleep.

13 There is a grievous evil *which* I have seen under the sun: riches being hoarded by their owner to his hurt.

14 When those riches were lost through a bad investment and he had fathered a son, then there was nothing to support him.

15 As he had come naked from his mother's womb, so will he return as he came. He will take nothing from the fruit of his labor that he can carry in his hand.

16 This also is a grievous evil—exactly as a man is born, thus will he die. So what is the advantage to him

who toils for the wind?

[17] Throughout his life *he* also eats in darkness with great vexation, sickness and anger.

[18] Here is what I have seen to be good and fitting: to eat, to drink and enjoy oneself in all one's labor in which he toils under the sun *during* the few years of his life which God has given him; for this is his reward.

[19] Furthermore, as for every man to whom God has given riches and wealth, He has also empowered him to eat from them and to receive his reward and rejoice in his labor; this is the gift of God.

[20] For he will not often consider the years of his life, because God keeps him occupied with the gladness of his heart.

Ecclesiastes 6

There is an evil which I have seen under the sun and it is prevalent among men—

2 a man to whom God has given riches and wealth and honor so that his soul lacks nothing of all that he desires; yet God has not empowered him to eat from them, for a foreigner enjoys them. This is vanity and a severe affliction.

3 If a man fathers a hundred *children* and lives many years, however many they be, but his soul is not satisfied with good things and he does not even have a *proper* burial, *then* I say, "Better the miscarriage than he,

4 for it comes in futility and goes into obscurity; and its name is covered in obscurity.

5 It never sees the sun and it never knows *anything*; it is better off than he.

6 Even if the *other* man lives a thousand years twice and does not enjoy good things—do not all go to one place?"

7 All a man's labor is for his mouth and yet the appetite is not satisfied.

8 For what advantage does the wise man have over the fool? What *advantage* does the poor man have, knowing *how* to walk before the living?

9 What the eyes see is better than what the soul desires. This too is futility and a striving after wind.

10 Whatever exists has already been named, and it is known what man is; for he cannot dispute with him who is stronger than he is.

11 For there are many words which increase futility. What *then* is the advantage to a man?

12 For who knows what is good for a man during *his* lifetime, *during* the few years of his futile life? He will spend them like a shadow. For who can tell a man what will be after him under the sun?

Ecclesiastes 7

A good name is better than a good ointment, And the day of *one's* death is better than the day of one's birth.

2 It is better to go to a house of mourning than to go to a house of feasting, Because that is the end of every man, And the living takes *it* to heart.

3 Sorrow is better than laughter, For when a face is sad a heart may be happy.

4 The mind of the wise is in the house of mourning, While the mind of fools is in the house of pleasure.

5 It is better to listen to the rebuke of a wise man than for one to listen to the song of fools.

6 For as the crackling of thorn bushes under a pot, So is the laughter of the fool; And this too is futility.

7 For oppression makes a wise man mad, And a bribe corrupts the heart.

8 The end of a matter is better than its beginning; Patience of spirit is better than haughtiness of spirit.

9 Do not be eager in your heart to be angry, For anger resides in the bosom of fools.

10 Do not say, "Why is it that the former days were better than these?" For it is not from wisdom that you ask about this.

11 Wisdom along with an inheritance is good And an advantage to those who see the sun.

12 For wisdom is protection *just as* money is protection, But the advantage of knowledge is that wisdom preserves the lives of its possessors.

13 Consider the work of God, For who is able to straighten what He has bent?

14 In the day of prosperity be happy, But in the day of adversity consider—God has made the one as well as the other So that man will not discover anything *that will be* after him.

15 I have seen everything during my lifetime of futility; there is a righteous man who perishes in his righteousness and there is a wicked man who prolongs *his life* in his wickedness.

16 Do not be excessively righteous and do not be overly wise. Why should you ruin yourself?

17 Do not be excessively wicked and do not be a fool. Why should you die before your time?

18 It is good that you grasp one thing and also not let go of the other; for the one who fears God comes forth with both of them.

Ecclesiastes – God's Game Plan

19 Wisdom strengthens a wise man more than ten rulers who are in a city.

20 Indeed, there is not a righteous man on earth who *continually* does good and who never sins. **A**

21 Also, do not take seriously all words which are spoken, so that you will not hear your servant cursing you.

22 For you also have realized that you likewise have many times cursed others.

23 I tested all this with wisdom, *and* I said, "I will be wise," but it was far from me.

24 What has been is remote and exceedingly mysterious. Who can discover it?

25 I directed my mind to know, to investigate and to seek wisdom and an explanation, and to know the evil of folly and the foolishness of madness.

26 And I discovered more bitter than death the woman whose heart is snares and nets, whose hands are chains. One who is pleasing to God will escape from her, but the sinner will be captured by her.

27 "Behold, I have discovered this," says the Preacher, "*adding* one thing to another to find an explanation,

28 which I am still seeking but have not found. I have found one man among a thousand, but I have not found a woman among all these.

29 Behold, I have found only this, that God made men upright, but they have sought out many devices."

Ecclesiastes 8

Who is like the wise man and who knows the interpretation of a matter? A man's wisdom illumines him and causes his stern face to beam.

2 I say, "Keep the command of the king because of the oath before God.

3 Do not be in a hurry to leave him. Do not join in an evil matter, for he will do whatever he pleases."

4 Since the word of the king is authoritative, who will say to him, "What are you doing?"

5 He who keeps a royal command experiences no trouble, for a wise heart knows the proper time and procedure.

6 For there is a proper time and procedure for every delight, though a man's trouble is heavy upon him.

7 If no one knows what will happen, who can tell him when it will happen?

8 No man has authority to restrain the wind with the wind, or authority over the day of death; and there is no discharge in the time of war, and evil will not deliver those who practice it.

9 All this I have seen and applied my mind to every deed that has been done under the sun wherein a man has exercised authority over another man to his hurt.

10 So then, I have seen the wicked buried, those who used to go in and out from the holy place, and they are soon forgotten in the city where they did thus. This too is futility.

11 Because the sentence against an evil deed is not executed quickly, therefore the hearts of the sons of men among them are given fully to do evil.

12 Although a sinner does evil a hundred times and may lengthen his life, still I know that it will be well for those who fear God, who fear Him openly. 13 But it will not be well for the evil man and he will not lengthen his days like a shadow, because he does not fear God.

14 There is futility which is done on the earth, that is, there are righteous men to whom it happens according to the deeds of the wicked. On the other hand, there are evil men to whom it happens according to the deeds of the righteous. I say that this too is futility.

15 So I commended pleasure, for there is nothing good for a man under the sun except to eat and to drink and to be merry, and this will stand by him in his toils throughout the days of his life which God has given him under the sun.

16 When I gave my heart to know wisdom and to see the task which has been done on the earth (even though one should never sleep day or night),

17 and I saw every work of God, I concluded that man cannot discover the work which has been done under the sun. Even though man should seek laboriously, he will not discover; and though the wise man should say, "I know," he cannot discover.

Ecclesiastes 9

For I have taken all this to my heart and explain it that righteous men, wise men, and their deeds are in the hand of God. Man does not know whether it will be love or hatred; anything awaits him.

2 It is the same for all. There is one fate for the righteous and for the wicked; for the good, for the clean and for the unclean; for the man who offers a sacrifice and for the one who does not sacrifice. As the good man is, so is the sinner; as the swearer is, so is the one who is afraid to swear.

Ecclesiastes – God's Game Plan

3 This is an evil in all that is done under the sun, that there is one fate for all men. Furthermore, the hearts of the sons of men are full of evil and insanity is in their hearts throughout their lives. Afterwards they go to the dead.

4 For whoever is joined with all the living, there is hope; surely a live dog is better than a dead lion.

5 For the living know they will die; but the dead do not know anything, nor have they any longer a reward, for their memory is forgotten.

6 Indeed their love, their hate and their zeal have already perished, and they will no longer have a share in all that is done under the sun.

7 Go then, eat your bread in happiness and drink your wine with a cheerful heart; for God has already approved your works.

8 Let your clothes be white all the time, and let not oil be lacking on your head.

9 Enjoy life with the woman whom you love all the days of your fleeting life which He has given to you under the sun; for this is your reward in life and in your toil in which you have labored under the sun. Whatever Your Hand Finds to Do

10 Whatever your hand finds to do, do it with all your might; for there is no activity or planning or knowledge or wisdom in Sheol where you are going.

11 I again saw under the sun that the race is not to the swift and the battle is not to the warriors, and neither is bread to the wise nor wealth to the discerning nor favor to men of ability; for time and chance overtake them all.

12 Moreover, man does not know his time: like fish caught in a treacherous net and birds trapped in a snare, so the sons of men are ensnared at an evil time when it suddenly falls on them.

13 Also this I came to see as wisdom under the sun, and it impressed me.

14 There was a small city with few men in it and a great king came to it, surrounded it and constructed large siegeworks against it.

15 But there was found in it a poor wise man and he delivered the city by his wisdom. Yet no one remembered that poor man.

16 So I said, "Wisdom is better than strength." But the wisdom of the poor man is despised and his words are not heeded.

17 The words of the wise heard in quietness are better than the shouting of a ruler among fools.

18 Wisdom is better than weapons of war, but one sinner destroys much good.

Ecclesiastes 10

Dead flies make a perfumer's oil stink, so a little foolishness is weightier than wisdom and honor.

2 A wise man's heart directs him toward the right, but the foolish man's heart directs him toward the left.

3 Even when the fool walks along the road, his sense is lacking and he demonstrates to everyone that he is a fool.

4 If the ruler's temper rises against you, do not abandon your position, because composure allays great offenses.

5 There is an evil I have seen under the sun, like an error which goes forth from the ruler—

6 folly is set in many exalted places while rich men sit in humble places.

7 I have seen slaves riding on horses and princes walking like slaves on the land.

8 He who digs a pit may fall into it, and a serpent may bite him who breaks through a wall.

9 He who quarries stones may be hurt by them, and he who splits logs may be endangered by them.

10 If the ax is dull and he does not sharpen its edge, then he must exert more strength. Wisdom has the advantage of giving success.

11 If the serpent bites before being charmed, there is no profit for the charmer. {*some versions read "A serpent may bite when it is not charmed, The babbler is no different.]* (babbler is rendered as "master of the tongue)

12 Words from the mouth of a wise man are gracious, while the lips of a fool consume him;

13 the beginning of his talking is folly and the end of it is wicked madness.

14 Yet the fool multiplies words. No man knows what will happen, and who can tell him what will come after him?

15 The toil of a fool so wearies him that he does not even know how to go to a city.

16 Woe to you, O land, whose king is a lad and whose princes feast in the morning.

17 Blessed are you, O land, whose king is of nobility and whose princes eat at the appropriate time—for

strength and not for drunkenness.

18 Through indolence the rafters sag, and through slackness the house leaks.

19 Men prepare a meal for enjoyment, and wine makes life merry, and money is the answer to everything.

20 Furthermore, in your bedchamber do not curse a king, and in your sleeping rooms do not curse a rich man, for a bird of the heavens will carry the sound and the winged creature will make the matter known.

Ecclesiastes 11

Cast your bread on the surface of the waters, for you will find it after many days.

2 Divide your portion to seven, or even to eight, for you do not know what misfortune may occur on the earth.

3 If the clouds are full, they pour out rain upon the earth; and whether a tree falls toward the south or toward the north, wherever the tree falls, there it lies.

4 He who watches the wind will not sow and he who looks at the clouds will not reap.

5 Just as you do not know the path of the wind and how bones are formed in the womb of the pregnant woman, so you do not know the activity of God who makes all things.

6 Sow your seed in the morning and do not be idle in the evening, for you do not know whether morning or evening sowing will succeed, or whether both of them alike will be good.

7 The light is pleasant, and it is good for the eyes to see the sun.

8 Indeed, if a man should live many years, let him rejoice in them all, and let him remember the days of darkness, for they will be many. Everything that is to come will be futility.

9 Rejoice, young man, during your childhood, and let your heart be pleasant during the days of young manhood. And follow the impulses of your heart and the desires of your eyes. Yet know that God will bring you to judgment for all these things.

10 So, remove grief and anger from your heart and put away pain from your body, because childhood and the prime of life are fleeting.

Ecclesiastes 12

Remember also your Creator in the days of your youth, before the evil days come and the years draw near when you will say, "I have no delight in them";

2 before the sun and the light, the moon and the stars are darkened, and clouds return after the rain;

3 in the day that the watchmen of the house tremble, and mighty men stoop, the grinding ones stand idle because they are few, and those who look through windows grow dim;

4 and the doors on the street are shut as the sound of the grinding mill is low, and one will arise at the sound of the bird, and all the daughters of song will sing softly.

5 Furthermore, men are afraid of a high place and of terrors on the road; the almond tree blossoms, the grasshopper drags himself along, and the caperberry is ineffective. For man goes to his eternal home while mourners go about in the street.

6 Remember Him before the silver cord is broken and the golden bowl is crushed, the pitcher by the well is shattered and the wheel at the cistern is crushed;

7 then the dust will return to the earth as it was, and the spirit will return to God who gave it.

8 "Vanity of vanities," says the Preacher, "all is vanity!"

9 In addition to being a wise man, the Preacher also taught the people knowledge; and he pondered, searched out and arranged many proverbs.

10 The Preacher sought to find delightful words and to write words of truth correctly.

11 The words of wise men are like goads, and masters of these collections are like well-driven nails; they are given by one Shepherd.

12 But beyond this, my son, be warned: the writing of many books is endless, and excessive devotion to books is wearying to the body.

13 The conclusion, when all has been heard, is: fear God and keep His commandments, because this applies to every person. 14 For God will bring every act to judgment, everything which is hidden, whether it is good or evil.

Appendix B

What is Vanity?

H1892 - hebel - Vanity/futility/emptiness, breath, vapor vanity

It occurs 37 times in 30 verses.

Striving after wind- occurs nine times. 8/9 occurs with the word vanity or futility

Scripture Location	What does it say? *(If you run out of space, use an additional sheet of paper)*

Appendix C

Under the Sun/Heaven

Under the sun/heaven is mentioned 33 times in 31 verses

Scripture Location	What does it say? *(If you run out of space, use an additional sheet of paper)*

Appendix D
Chapter 1 Cross References

Proverbs 1:7 (NASB)

7 The fear of the Lord is the beginning of knowledge; Fools despise wisdom and instruction.

Proverbs 2:6 (NASB)

6 For the Lord gives wisdom; From His mouth *come* knowledge and understanding.

Proverbs 9:10 (NASB)

10 The fear of the Lord is the beginning of wisdom, and the knowledge of the Holy One is understanding.

Proverbs 15:33 (NASB)

33 The fear of the Lord is the instruction for wisdom, and before honor *comes* humility.

1 Corinthians 1:18-25 (MSG)

18-21 The Message that points to Christ on the Cross seems like sheer silliness to those hell-bent on destruction, but for those on the way of salvation it makes perfect sense. This is the way God works, and most powerfully as it turns out. It's written,

I'll turn conventional wisdom on its head;
I'll expose so-called experts as crackpots.

So where can you find someone truly wise, truly educated, truly intelligent in this day and age? Hasn't God exposed it all as pretentious nonsense? Since the world in all its fancy wisdom never had a clue when it came to knowing God, God in his wisdom took delight in using what the world considered dumb—*preaching*, of all things!—to bring those who trust him into the way of salvation.

22-25 While Jews clamor for miraculous demonstrations and Greeks go in for philosophical wisdom, we go right on proclaiming Christ, the Crucified. Jews treat this like an *anti*-miracle—and Greeks pass it off as absurd. But to us who are personally called by God himself—both Jews and Greeks—Christ is God's ultimate miracle and wisdom all wrapped up in one. Human wisdom is so tinny, so impotent, next to the seeming absurdity of God. Human strength can't begin to compete with God's "weakness."

Chapter 2 Cross References

Proverbs 30:7-9 (NASB)

7 Two things I asked of You, Do not refuse me before I die:

8 Keep deception and lies far from me, Give me neither poverty nor riches; Feed me with the food that is my portion,

9 That I not be full and deny *You* and say, "Who is the Lord?" Or that I not be in want and steal, And profane the name of my God.

Chapter 3 Cross References

Proverbs 25:2 (NLV)

It is the greatness of God to keep things hidden, but it is the greatness of kings to find things out.

1 Corinthians 2:6-16(NASB)

6 Yet we do speak wisdom among those who are mature; a wisdom, however, not of this age nor of the rulers of this age, who are passing away; 7 but we speak God's wisdom in a mystery, the hidden *wisdom* which God predestined before the ages to our glory; 8 *the wisdom* which none of the rulers of this age has understood; for if they had understood it they would not have crucified the Lord of glory; 9 but just as it is written,

"Things which eye has not seen and ear has not heard,
And which have not entered the heart of man,
all that God has prepared for those who love Him."

10 For to us God revealed *them* through the Spirit; for the Spirit searches all things, even the depths of God. 11 For who among men knows the *thoughts* of a man except the spirit of the man which is in him? Even so the *thoughts* of God no one knows except the Spirit of God. 12 Now we have received, not the spirit of the world, but the Spirit who is from God, so that we may know the things freely given to us by God, 13 which things we also speak, not in words taught by human wisdom, but in those taught by the Spirit, combining spiritual *thoughts* with spiritual *words*.

14 But a natural man does not accept the things of the Spirit of God, for they are foolishness to him; and

he cannot understand them, because they are spiritually appraised. 15 But he who is spiritual appraises all things, yet he himself is appraised by no one. 16 *For who has known the mind of the Lord, that he will instruct Him?* But we have the mind of Christ.

Appendix E
Cross References for Chapter 3

Mark 4:10-13 NASB

As soon as He was alone, His followers, along with the twelve, began asking Him about the parables.

And He was saying to them, "To you has been given the mystery of the kingdom of God, but those who are outside get everything in parables,

so that WHILE SEEING, THEY MAY SEE AND NOT PERCEIVE, AND WHILE HEARING, THEY MAY HEAR AND NOT UNDERSTAND, OTHERWISE THEY MIGHT RETURN AND BE FORGIVEN." And He said to them, "Do you not understand this parable? How will you understand all the parables?

Romans 14:10-15 (NASB)

10 But you, why do you judge your brother? Or you again, why do you regard your brother with contempt? For we will all stand before the judgment seat of God. 11 For it is written,

"As I live, says the Lord, every knee shall bow to Me,

And every tongue shall give praise to God."

12 So then each one of us will give an account of himself to God.

13 Therefore let us not judge one another anymore, but rather determine this—not to put an obstacle or a stumbling block in a brother's way. 14 I know and am convinced in the Lord Jesus that nothing is unclean in itself; but to him who thinks anything to be unclean, to him it is unclean. 15 For if because of food your brother is hurt, you are no longer walking according to love. Do not destroy with your food him for whom Christ died.

1 Corinthians 4:5 (NASB)

[5] Therefore do not go on passing judgment before the time, *but wait* until the Lord comes who will both bring to light the things hidden in the darkness and disclose the motives of *men's* hearts; and then each man's praise will come to him from God.

Ecclesiastes – God's Game Plan

Matthew 8:29 (NASB)

[29] And they cried out, saying, "What business do we have with each other, Son of God? Have You come here to torment us before the time?"

Appendix F
Cross References for Chapter 4

John 14:16; 26 (KJV)

16 And I will pray the Father, and he shall give you another Comforter, that he may abide with you forever;

26 But the Comforter, which is the Holy Ghost, whom the Father will send in my name, he shall teach you all things, and bring all things to your remembrance, whatsoever I have said unto you.

John 15:26 (KJV)

But when the Comforter is come, whom I will send unto you from the Father, even the Spirit of truth, which proceedeth from the Father, he shall testify of me:

John 16:7-8 (KJV)

7 Nevertheless I tell you the truth; it is expedient for you that I go away: for if I go not away, the Comforter will not come unto you; but if I depart, I will send him unto you.

8 And when he is come, he will reprove the world of sin, and of righteousness, and of judgment:

Proverbs 17:17 (GW)

17 A friend always loves and a brother is born to share trouble.

Proverbs 18:24 (NASB)

24 A man of too many friends comes to ruin, but there is a friend who sticks closer than a brother.

Appendix G
Cross References for Chapter 5

Psalm 122:1 (NASB)

I was glad when they said to me, "Let us go to the house of the Lord."

Numbers 30:2 (NASB)

If a man vows a vow to the Lord, or swears an oath to bind himself by a pledge, he shall not break his word. He shall do according to all that proceeds out of his mouth.

Deuteronomy 23:21-23 (NASB)

"If you make a vow to the Lord your God, you shall not delay fulfilling it, for the Lord your God will surely require it of you, and you will be guilty of sin. But if you refrain from vowing, you will not be guilty of sin. You shall be careful to do what has passed your lips, for you have voluntarily vowed to the Lord your God what you have promised with your mouth.

Psalm 66:13- 14 (NASB)

I will come into your house with burnt offerings; I will perform my vows to you, that which my lips uttered and my mouth promised when I was in trouble.

Proverbs 20:25 (NASB)

It is a snare to say rashly, "It is holy," and to reflect only after making vows.

Matthew 5:33-35 (NASB)

"Again you have heard that it was said to those of old, 'You shall not swear falsely, but shall perform to the Lord what you have sworn.' But I say to you, do not take an oath at all, either by heaven, for it is the throne of God, or by the earth, for it is his footstool, or by Jerusalem, for it is the city of the great King. And do not take an oath by your head, for you cannot make one hair white or black. Let what you say be simply 'Yes' or 'No'; anything more than this comes from evil.

Romans 12:1-2 (NASB)

I appeal to you therefore, brothers, by the mercies of God, to present your bodies as a living sacrifice, holy and acceptable to God, which is your spiritual worship. Do not be conformed to this world, but be transformed by the renewal of your mind, that by testing you may discern what is the will of God, what is good and acceptable and perfect.

Job 1:21 (NASB)

21 {Job} said, "Naked I came from my mother's womb, and naked I shall return there. The Lord gave and the Lord has taken away. Blessed be the name of the Lord."

Matthew 6:19-21, 24 (NASB)

19 "Do not store up for yourselves treasures on earth, where moth and rust destroy, and where thieves break in and steal. 20 But store up for yourselves treasures in heaven, where neither moth nor rust destroys, and where thieves do not break in or steal; 21 for where your treasure is, there your heart will be also…24 "No one can serve two masters; for either he will hate the one and love the other, or he will be devoted to one and despise the other. You cannot serve God and wealth.

1 Timothy 6:6-10 (NASB)

6 But godliness *actually* is a means of great gain when accompanied by contentment. 7 For we have brought nothing into the world, so we cannot take anything out of it either. 8 If we have food and covering, with these we shall be content. 9 But those who want to get rich fall into temptation and a snare and many foolish and harmful desires which plunge men into ruin and destruction. 10 For the love of money is a root of all sorts of evil, and some by longing for it have wandered away from the faith and pierced themselves with many griefs.

Hebrews 13:5-6 (MSG)

Ecclesiastes – God's Game Plan

5-6 Don't be obsessed with getting more material things. Be relaxed with what you have. Since God assured us, "I'll never let you down, never walk off and leave you," we can boldly quote,

God is there, ready to help; I'm fearless no matter what. Who or what can get to me?

Appendix H
Cross References for Chapter 6
Psalm 139:16 (NLV)

16 Your eyes saw me before I was put together. And all the days of my life were written in Your book before any of them came to be.

Proverbs 20:24 (GW)

24 The Lord is the one who directs a person's steps. How then can anyone understand his own way?

Romans 8:28-30 (GW)

28 We know that all things work together for the good of those who love God—those whom he has called according to his plan. 29 This is true because he already knew his people and had already appointed them to have the same form as the image of his Son. Therefore, his Son is the firstborn among many children. 30 He also called those whom he had already appointed. He approved of those whom he had called, and he gave glory to those whom he had approved of.

Psalm 39:5 (GW)

5 Indeed, you have made the length of my days only a few inches. My lifespan is nothing compared to yours. Certainly, everyone alive is like a whisper in the wind. Selah

Psalm 144:3-4 (NASB)

3 O LORD, what is man, that You take knowledge of him? Or the son of man, that You think of him?
4 Man is like a mere breath; His days are like a passing shadow.

James 4:14 (NASB)

14]Yet you do not know [fn]what your life will be like tomorrow. You are *just* a vapor that appears for a little while and then vanishes away.

Appendix I
Cross References for Chapter 7

Exodus 23:8 (NASB)

8 "You shall not take a bribe, for a bribe blinds the clear-sighted and subverts the cause of the just...

Matthew 28:12-15 (NASB)

12 And when they had assembled with the elders and consulted together, they gave a large sum of money to the soldiers, 13 and said, "You are to say, 'His disciples came by night and stole Him away while we were asleep.' 14 And if this should come to the governor's ears, we will win him over and keep you out of trouble." 15 And they took the money and did as they had been instructed; and this story was widely spread among the Jews, *and is* to this day.

Luke 3:12-14 (NASB)

12 And *some* tax collectors also came to be baptized, and they said to him *(John the Baptist)*, "Teacher, what shall we do?" 13 And he said to them, "Collect no more than what you have been ordered to." 14 *Some* soldiers were questioning him, saying, "And *what about* us, what shall we do?" And he said to them, "Do not take money from anyone by force, or accuse *anyone* falsely, and be content with your wages."

Mark 14:9-11 (NASB)

9 Truly I say to you, wherever the gospel is preached in the whole world, what this woman has done will also be spoken of in memory of her."

10 Then Judas Iscariot, who was one of the twelve, went off to the chief priests in order to betray Him to them. 11 They were glad when they heard *this*, and promised to give him money. And he *began* seeking how to betray Him at an opportune time.

Proverbs 15:26-28 (NASB)

26 Evil plans are an abomination to the Lord, But pleasant words are pure.

27 He who profits illicitly troubles his own house, But he who hates bribes will live.

Psalm 15 (NASB)

O Lord, who may abide in Your tent? Who may dwell on Your holy hill?

2 He who walks with integrity, and works righteousness, And speaks truth in his heart.

3 He does not slander with his tongue, Nor does evil to his neighbor, Nor takes up a reproach against his friend;

4 In whose eyes a reprobate is despised, But who honors those who fear the Lord; He swears to his own hurt and does not change;

5 He does not put out his money at interest, Nor does he take a bribe against the innocent. He who does these things will never be shaken.

Proverbs 29:11 (NASB)

11 A fool always loses his temper, But a wise man holds it back.

Proverbs 16:32 (NASB)

32 He who is slow to anger is better than the mighty, And he who rules his spirit, than he who captures a city.

James 1:19-20 (NASB)

19 *This* you know, my beloved brethren. But everyone must be quick to hear, slow to speak *and* slow to anger; 20 for the anger of man does not achieve the righteousness of God.

1 Samuel 2:6-8 (NLV)

6 The Lord kills and brings to life. He brings down to the grave, and He raises up. 7 The Lord makes poor and makes rich. He brings low and He lifts up. 8 He lifts the poor from the dust. He lifts those in need

from the ashes. He makes them sit with rulers and receive a seat of honor. For what holds the earth belongs to the Lord. He has set the world in its place.

Job 2:10 (NASB)

10 But he said to her, "You speak as one of the foolish women speaks. Shall we indeed accept good from God and not accept adversity?" In all this Job did not sin with his lips.

Ecclesiastes 3:22 (NASB)

22 I have seen that nothing is better than that man should be happy in his activities, for that is his lot. For who will bring him to see what will occur after him?

James 1:2-4 (NASB)

2 Consider it all joy, my brethren, when you encounter various trials, 3 knowing that the testing of your faith produces endurance. 4 And let endurance have *its* perfect result, so that you may be perfect and complete, lacking in nothing.

Proverbs 1:7 (NASB)

7 The fear of the Lord is the beginning of knowledge; Fools despise wisdom and instruction.

Proverbs 2:10-11(NASB)

10 For wisdom will enter your heart And knowledge will be pleasant to your soul;

11 Discretion will guard you, Understanding will watch over you…

Proverbs 2:16-17 (NASB)

16 To deliver you from the strange woman,

From the adulteress who flatters with her words;

17 That leaves the companion of her youth

And forgets the covenant of her God;

18 For her house sinks down to death

And her tracks *lead* to the dead;

Genesis 1:26-27 (NASB)

26 Then God said, "Let Us make man in Our image, according to Our likeness; and let them rule over the fish of the sea and over the birds of the sky and over the cattle and over all the earth, and over every creeping thing that creeps on the earth." 27 God created man in His own image, in the image of God He created him; male and female He created them.

Genesis 6:5-7 (MSG)

5-7 God saw that human evil was out of control. People thought evil, imagined evil—evil, evil, evil from morning to night. God was sorry that he had made the human race in the first place; it broke his heart. God said, "I'll get rid of my ruined creation, make a clean sweep: people, animals, snakes and bugs, birds—the works. I'm sorry I made them."

1 Corinthians 5:1-2 (NLV)

5 Someone has told me about a sex sin among you. It is so bad that even the people who do not know God would not do it. I have been told that one of the men is living with his father's wife as if she were his wife. 2 Instead of being sorry, you are proud of yourselves. The man who is living like that should be sent away from you

Appendix J
Chapter 8 Cross References

2 Samuel 12:1-9, 13 (NASB)

2Sa 12:1 Then the LORD sent Nathan to David. And he came to him and said, "There were two men in one city, the one rich and the other poor.

2Sa 12:2 "The rich man had a great many flocks and herds.

2Sa 12:3 "But the poor man had nothing except one little ewe lamb Which he bought and nourished; And it grew up together with him and his children. It would eat of his bread and drink of his cup and lie in his bosom, And was like a daughter to him.

2Sa 12:4 "Now a traveler came to the rich man, And he was unwilling to take from his own flock or his own herd, To prepare for the wayfarer who had come to him; Rather he took the poor man's ewe lamb and prepared it for the man who had come to him."

2Sa 12:5 Then David's anger burned greatly against the man, and he said to Nathan, "As the LORD lives, surely the man who has done this deserves to die.

2Sa 12:6 "He must make restitution for the lamb fourfold, because he did this thing and had no compassion."

2Sa 12:7 Nathan then said to David, "You are the man! Thus says the LORD God of Israel, 'It is I who anointed you king over Israel and it is I who delivered you from the hand of Saul.

2Sa 12:8 'I also gave you your master's house and your master's wives into your care, and I gave you the house of Israel and Judah; and if that had been too little, I would have added to you many more things like these!

2Sa 12:9 'Why have you despised the word of the LORD by doing evil in His sight? You have struck down Uriah the Hittite with the sword, have taken his wife to be your wife, and have killed him with the sword of the sons of Ammon.

2Sa 12:13 Then David said to Nathan, "I have sinned against the LORD." And Nathan said to David, "The LORD also has taken away your sin; you shall not die.

1 Timothy 5:19 (MSG)

19 Don't listen to a complaint against a leader that isn't backed up by two or three responsible witnesses.

Romans 5:12-17 (NASB)

12 Therefore, just as through one man sin entered into the world, and death through sin, and so death spread to all men, because all sinned— 13 for until the Law sin was in the world, but sin is not imputed when there is no law. 14 Nevertheless death reigned from Adam until Moses, even over those who had not sinned in the likeness of the offense of Adam, who is a type of Him who was to come.

15 But the free gift is not like the transgression. For if by the transgression of the one the many died, much more did the grace of God and the gift by the grace of the one Man, Jesus Christ, abound to the many. 16 The gift is not like *that which came* through the one who sinned; for on the one hand the judgment *arose* from one *transgression* resulting in condemnation, but on the other hand the free gift *arose* from many transgressions resulting in justification. 17 For if by the transgression of the one, death reigned through the one, much more those who receive the abundance of grace and of the gift of righteousness will reign in life through the One, Jesus Christ.

Hebrews 9:27-28 (NASB)

27 And inasmuch as it is appointed for men to die once and after this *comes* judgment, 28 so Christ also, having been offered once to bear the sins of many, will appear a second time for salvation without *reference to* sin, to those who eagerly await Him.

Psalm 37:7 (NASB)

Rest in the Lord and wait patiently for Him; Do not fret because of him who **prosper**s in his way, Because of the man who carries out **wicked** schemes.

Psalm 73 (NASB)

Surely God is good to Israel, To those who are pure in heart!

2 But as for me, my feet came close to stumbling, My steps had almost slipped.

3 For I was envious of the arrogant *As* I saw the prosperity of the wicked.

4 For there are no pains in their death, And their body is fat.

Ecclesiastes – God's Game Plan

5 They are not in trouble *as other* men, Nor are they plagued like mankind.

6 Therefore pride is their necklace; The garment of violence covers them.

7 Their eye bulges from fatness; The imaginations of *their* heart run riot.

8 They mock and wickedly speak of oppression; They speak from on high.

9 They have set their mouth against the heavens, And their tongue parades through the earth.

10 Therefore his people return to this place, And waters of abundance are drunk by them.

11 They say, "How does God know? And is there knowledge with the Most High?"

12 Behold, these are the wicked; And always at ease, they have increased *in* wealth.

13 Surely in vain I have kept my heart pure And washed my hands in innocence;

14 For I have been stricken all day long And chastened every morning.

15 If I had said, "I will speak thus," Behold, I would have betrayed the generation of Your children.

16 When I pondered to understand this, It was troublesome in my sight

17 Until I came into the sanctuary of God; *Then* I perceived their end.

18 Surely You set them in slippery places; You cast them down to destruction.

19 How they are destroyed in a moment! They are utterly swept away by sudden terrors!

20 Like a dream when one awakes, O Lord, when aroused, You will despise their form.

21 When my heart was embittered And I was pierced within,

22 Then I was senseless and ignorant; I was *like* a beast before You.

23 Nevertheless I am continually with You; You have taken hold of my right hand.

24 With Your counsel You will guide me, And afterward receive me to glory.

25 Whom have I in heaven *but You*? And besides You, I desire nothing on earth.

26 My flesh and my heart may fail; But God is the strength of my heart and my portion forever.

27 For, behold, those who are far from You will perish; You have destroyed all those who are unfaithful to You.

28 But as for me, the nearness of God is my good; I have made the Lord God my refuge, That I may tell of all Your works.

Psalm 40:5 (NCV)

5 Lord my God, you have done many miracles.
Your plans for us are many.

If I tried to tell them all,

there would be too many to count.

John 21:24-25 (NASB)

24 This is the disciple who is testifying to these things and wrote these things, and we know that his testimony is true.

25 And there are also many other things which Jesus did, which if they *were written in detail, I suppose that even the world itself *would not contain the books that *would be written.

Philippians 4:10-13 (NASB)

10 But I rejoiced in the Lord greatly, that now at last you have revived your concern for me; indeed, you were concerned *before*, but you lacked opportunity. 11 Not that I speak from want, for I have learned to be content in whatever circumstances I am. 12 I know how to get along with humble means, and I also know how to live in prosperity; in any and every circumstance I have learned the secret of being filled and going hungry, both of having abundance and suffering need. 13 I can do all things through Him who strengthens me.

Appendix K
Chapter 9 Cross References

1 Corinthians 6:9-11 (NASB)

9 Or do you not know that the unrighteous will not inherit the kingdom of God? Do not be deceived; neither fornicators, nor idolaters, nor adulterers, nor effeminate, nor homosexuals, 10 nor thieves, nor *the* covetous, nor drunkards, nor revilers, nor swindlers, will inherit the kingdom of God. 11 Such were some of you; but you were washed, but you were sanctified, but you were justified in the name of the Lord Jesus Christ and in the Spirit of our God.

Galatians 5:19-21 (NASB)

19 Now the deeds of the flesh are evident, which are: immorality, impurity, sensuality, 20 idolatry, sorcery, enmities, strife, jealousy, outbursts of anger, disputes, dissensions, factions, 21 envying, drunkenness, carousing, and things like these, of which I forewarn you, just as I have forewarned you, that those who practice such things will not inherit the kingdom of God.

Ephesians 5:5 (GW)

5 You know very well that no person who is involved in sexual sin, perversion, or greed (which means worshiping wealth) can have any inheritance in the kingdom of Christ and of God.

Galatians 6:7-8 (NASB)

7 Do not be deceived, God is not mocked; for whatever a man sows, this he will also reap. 8 For the one who sows to his own flesh will from the flesh reap corruption, but the one who sows to the Spirit will from the Spirit reap eternal life.

Proverbs 22:29 (NASB)

29 Do you see a man skilled in his work?

He will stand before kings;

He will not stand before obscure men.

1 Corinthians 15:57-58 (NASB)

57 but thanks be to God, who gives us the victory through our Lord Jesus Christ.

58 Therefore, my beloved brethren, be steadfast, immovable, always abounding in the work of the Lord, knowing that your toil is not *in* vain in the Lord.

Colossians 3:23-25 (NASB)

23 Whatever you do, do your work heartily, as for the Lord rather than for men, 24 knowing that from the Lord you will receive the reward of the inheritance. It is the Lord Christ whom you serve. 25 For he who does wrong will receive the consequences of the wrong which he has done, and that without partiality.

Proverbs 14:20 (NASB)

20 The poor is hated even by his neighbor, But those who love the rich are many.

Proverbs 19:7 (NCV)

7 Poor people's relatives avoid them; even their friends stay far away. They run after them, begging, but they are gone.

James 2:6 (NASB)

6 But you have dishonored the poor man. Is it not the rich who oppress you and personally drag you into court?

Romans 2:10-11 (NASB)

10 but glory and honor and peace to everyone who does good, to the Jew first and also to the Greek. 11 For there is no partiality with God.

Ephesians 5:15-17 (GW)

15 So then, be very careful how you live. Don't live like foolish people but likewise people. 16 Make the most of your opportunities because these are evil days. 17 So don't be foolish, but understand what the Lord wants.

Joshua 7:1, 5, 7, 10-12, 20-21, 25 (NASB)

1 But the sons of Israel acted unfaithfully in regard to the things under the ban, for Achan, the son of Carmi, the son of Zabdi, the son of Zerah, from the tribe of Judah, took some of the things under the ban, therefore the anger of the LORD burned against the sons of Israel....

5 The men of Ai struck down about thirty-six of their men, and pursued them from the gate as far as Shebarim and struck them down on the descent, so the hearts of the people melted and became as water…

7 Joshua said, "Alas, O Lord GOD, why did You ever bring this people over the Jordan, only to deliver us into the hand of the Amorites, to destroy us? If only we had been willing to dwell beyond the Jordan!...

10 So the LORD said to Joshua, "Rise up! Why is it that you have fallen on your face? 11 "Israel has sinned, and they have also transgressed My covenant which I commanded them. And they have even taken some of the things under the ban and have both stolen and deceived. Moreover, they have also put them among their own things. 12 "Therefore the sons of Israel cannot stand before their enemies; they turn their backs before their enemies, for they have become accursed. I will not be with you anymore unless you destroy the things under the ban from your midst....

20 So Achan answered Joshua and said, "Truly, I have sinned against the LORD, the God of Israel, and this is what I did: 21 when I saw among the spoil a beautiful mantle from Shinar and two hundred shekels of silver and a bar of gold fifty shekels in weight, then I coveted them and took them; and behold, they are concealed in the earth inside my tent with the silver underneath it."...

25 Joshua said, "Why have you troubled us? The LORD will trouble you this day." And all Israel stoned them with stones; and they burned them with fire after they had stoned them with stones.

1 Kings 11:4 (NASB)

4 For when Solomon was old, his wives turned his heart away after other gods; and his heart was not wholly devoted to the Lord his God, as the heart of David his father *had been*.

1 Corinthians 15:33

GOD'S WORD Translation (GW)

33 Don't let anyone deceive you. Associating with bad people will ruin decent people.

Appendix L
Chapter 10 Cross References

Luke 12:1-3 (NCV)

12 So many thousands of people had gathered that they were stepping on each other. Jesus spoke first to his followers, saying, "Beware of the yeast of the Pharisees, because they are hypocrites. 2 Everything that is hidden will be shown, and everything that is secret will be made known. 3 What you have said in the dark will be heard in the light, and what you have whispered in an inner room will be shouted from the housetops.

1 Corinthians 5:6-8 (MSG)

6-8 Your flip and callous arrogance in these things bothers me. You pass it off as a small thing, but it's anything but that. Yeast, too, is a "small thing," but it works its way through a whole batch of bread dough pretty fast. So get rid of this "yeast." Our true identity is flat and plain, not puffed up with the wrong kind of ingredient. The Messiah, our Passover Lamb, has already been sacrificed for the Passover meal, and we are the Unraised Bread part of the Feast. So let's live out our part in the Feast, not as raised bread swollen with the yeast of evil, but as flatbread—simple, genuine, unpretentious.

Proverbs 6:10-11 (GW)

10 "Just a little sleep, just a little slumber, just a little nap."

11 Then your poverty will come to you like a drifter, and your need will come to you like a bandit.

Proverbs 19:10 (NASB)

10 Luxury is not fitting for a fool; Much less for a slave to rule over princes.

Proverbs 30:21-22 (NASB)

21 Under three things the earth quakes, And under four, it cannot bear up:

22 Under a slave when he becomes king, And a fool when he is satisfied with food,

Proverbs 25:15 (NLV)

15 When one is slow to anger, a ruler may be won over. A gentle tongue will break a bone.

Jeremiah 8:17 (NASB)

"For behold, I am sending serpents against you, Adders, for which there is no charm,

And they will bite you," declares the Lord.

Psalm 58:3-6 (NASB)

Even inside the womb wicked people are strangers to God. From their birth liars go astray.

4 They have poisonous venom like snakes. They are like a deaf cobra that shuts its ears

5 so that it cannot hear the voice of a snake charmer or of anyone trained to cast spells.

6 O God, knock the teeth out of their mouths.

Song of Solomon 2:15 (NCV)

15 Catch the foxes for us— the little foxes that ruin the vineyards while they are in blossom.

Proverbs 10:32 (NLT)

32 The lips of the godly speak helpful words, but the mouth of the wicked speaks perverse words.

Proverbs 18:7 (NASB)

7 A fool's mouth is his ruin, And his lips are the snare of his soul.

Proverbs 24:30-34 (NLV)

30 I passed by the field of the lazy man, by the grapevines of the man without understanding. 31 And see, it was all grown over with thorns. The ground was covered with weeds, and its stone wall was broken down. 32 When I saw it, I thought about it. I looked and received teaching. 33 "A little sleep, a little rest, a little folding of the hands to rest," 34 and your being poor will come as a robber, and your need like a man ready to fight.

Ecclesiastes – God's Game Plan

Colossians 4:6 (NASB)

6 Let your speech always be with grace, *as though* seasoned with salt, so that you will know how you should respond to each person.

Mark 9:50 (NASB)

50 Salt is good; but if the salt becomes unsalty, with what will you make it salty *again*? Have salt in yourselves, and be at peace with one another

Matthew 5:13 (NASB)

13 "You are the salt of the earth; but if the salt has become tasteless, how can it be made salty *again*? It is no longer good for anything, except to be thrown out and trampled underfoot by men.

Appendix M
Chapter 11 Cross References

Deuteronomy 15:10-11 (NASB)

10 You shall generously give to him, and your heart shall not be grieved when you give to him, because for this thing the Lord your God will bless you in all your work and in all your undertakings. 11 For the poor will never cease to be in the land; therefore I command you, saying, 'You shall freely open your hand to your brother, to your needy and poor in your land.'

Proverbs 19:17 (NASB)

17 One who is gracious to a poor man lends to the Lord, And He will repay him for his good deed.

Matthew 10:42 (NASB)

42 "And whoever in the name of a disciple gives to one of these [fn]little ones even a cup of cold water to drink, truly I say to you, he shall not lose his reward."

2 Corinthians 9:8-12 (NASB)

8 And God is able to make all grace abound to you, so that always having all sufficiency in everything, you may have an abundance for every good deed; 9 as it is written,

"He scattered abroad, he gave to the poor, His righteousness endures forever." (Psalm 112:9)

10 Now He who supplies seed to the sower and bread for food will supply and multiply your seed for sowing and increase the harvest of your righteousness; 11 you will be enriched in everything for all liberality, which through us is producing thanksgiving to God. 12 For the ministry of this service is not only fully supplying the needs of the saints, but is also overflowing through many thanksgivings to God.

Ecclesiastes 9:10 (NCV)

10 Whatever work you do, do your best, because you are going to the grave, where there is no working, no planning, no knowledge, and no wisdom.

Ecclesiastes – God's Game Plan

Psalm 115:17-18 (NASB)

17 The dead do not praise the LORD, nor *do* any who go down into silence;

18But as for us, we will bless the LORD From this time forth and forever. Praise the LORD!

John 9:4-5 (NCV)

4 While it is daytime, we must continue doing the work of the One who sent me. Night is coming, when no one can work. 5 While I am in the world, I am the light of the world."

Appendix N

Ecclesiastes 11:1-2

Cast your bread on the surface of the waters, for you will find it after many days.

[2] Divide your portion to seven, or even to eight, for you do not know what misfortune may occur on the earth.

Directions: Name 7-8 different things you can sow to be a blessing (ex: I can sow my time into a homeless shelter. I can sow my words of kindness into someone…).

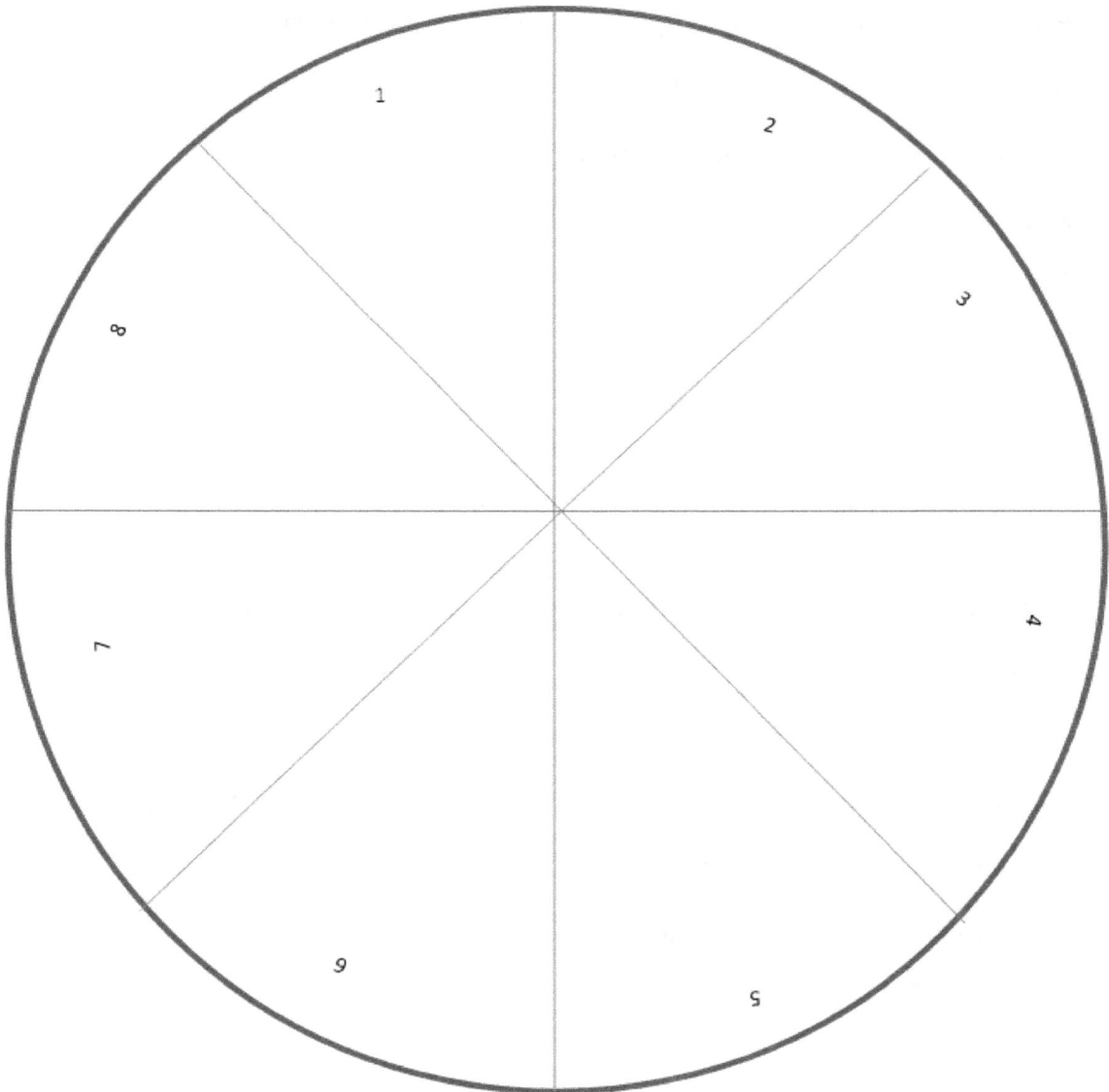

Appendix O

Five Questions to Discover Solomon's Purpose

1. What main thing did Solomon see in society that burdened or grieved him?

2. What group of people was he passionate about? (Circle one)

   People in general   Children   Couples   Professionals

   Adults   Teens   Families   Religious groups

   An ethnic group   Women   Singles   Non-Christians

   Seniors   Men   Single-family households

   Other_____

3. What was his message to this group? (His Objective)

4. Choose words of how he wanted to help the above group (circle two)

Motivate	Create	Discover
Encourage	Comfort	Lead
Empower	Influence	Impact
Nurture	Impart	Repair
Challenge	Equip	Change
Serve	Develop	Organize
Other		

1. What did he want this above group to become as a result of his influence?

   Examples:

   - To live a successful life

   - To be productive

   - Maximize their potential

   - To obtain more out of their lives

   - To reach higher goals

   - Other-

The Purpose Code

Take the answers to the questions and follow the Code: 4,2,3,5

4.

2.

3.

5.

Example: *Solomon's purpose was to teach people who were living below their potential how to understand who they are in God and what He said about their life by equipping them with tools to gain a biblical understanding so they will be passionate and purposeful in applying God's word to their life.*

Solomon's purpose was:

Ecclesiastes – God's Game Plan

Find his field

1. Home

2. Education

3. Business

4. Gov't

5. Medical

6. The Arts-Media, Technology, Music

7. Ministry

8. Land/Community

Appendix P
Chapter 12 Cross References

Proverbs 1:1-6 (NLV)

1 These are the wise sayings of Solomon, son of David, king of Israel: 2 They show you how to know wisdom and teaching, to find the words of understanding. 3 They help you learn about the ways of wisdom and what is right and fair. 4 They give wisdom to the child-like, and much learning and wisdom to those who are young. 5 A wise man will hear and grow in learning. A man of understanding will become able 6 to understand a saying and a picture-story, the words of the wise and what they mean

Acts 26:13-15 (NASB)

at midday, O King, I saw on the way a light from heaven, brighter than the sun, shining all around me and those who were journeying with me. 14 And when we had all fallen to the ground, I heard a voice saying to me in the Hebrew dialect, 'Saul, Saul, why are you persecuting Me? It is hard for you to kick against the goads.' 15 And I said, 'Who are You, Lord?' And the Lord said, 'I am Jesus whom you are persecuting.

1 Kings 4:30-32 (NASB)

Solomon's wisdom surpassed the wisdom of all the sons of the east and all the wisdom of Egypt. 31 For he was wiser than all men…and his fame was known in all the surrounding nations. 32 He also spoke 3,000 proverbs, and his songs were 1,005.

Ecclesiastes 1:18 (NASB)

18 Because in much wisdom there is much grief, and increasing knowledge results in increasing pain.

Appendix Q

Five Questions to Discover Your Purpose

1. What main thing do you see in society that burdens or grieves you? (this issue must elicit a response of anger, grief, or sadness. It should compel you to want to act to fix it)

2. What group of people are you passionate about? (Circle one)

   People in general   Children   Couples   Professionals

   Adults   Teens   Families   Religious groups

   An ethnic group   Women   Singles   Non-Christians

   Seniors   Men   Single-family households

   Other_____

3. What would be your message to this group? (Your Objective)

4. Choose words of how you want to help the above group (circle two)

Motivate	Create	Discover
Encourage	Comfort	Lead
Empower	Influence	Impact
Nurture	Impart	Repair
Challenge	Equip	Change
Serve	Develop	Organize
Other		

5. What do you want this above group to become as a result of your influence?

Examples:

- To live a successful life

- To be productive

- Maximize their potential

- To obtain more out of their lives

- To reach higher goals

- Other-

The Purpose Code

Take the answers to the questions and follow the Code: 4,2,3,5

4.

2.

3.

5.

Example: *Laura's purpose is to teach people who are living below their potential how to understand who they are in God and what He says about their life by equipping them with tools to gain a biblical understanding so they will be passionate and purposeful in applying God's word to their life.*

My Purpose is:

Ecclesiastes – God's Game Plan

Find your field

1. Home

2. Education

3. Business

4. Government

5. Medical

6. The Arts-Media, Technology, Music

7. Ministry

8. Land/Community

Appendix R

How to Use a PICK Chart

By Miles Jarvis, eHow Contributor

A PICK Chart is a Lean Six Sigma idea-evaluating tool.

PICK charts are used in business environments to help groups evaluate, categorize and compare multiple improvement ideas to decide which ideas to implement. Ideas are assessed according to four characteristics represented on the two axes of the chart, creating four quadrants. The four characteristics are: high payoff, low payoff, hard to do, and easy to do. These create four categories that correspond with the letters of the acronym "PICK": Possible (low payoff, easy to do), Implement (high payoff, easy to do), Challenge (high payoff, hard to do), and Kill (low payoff, hard to do).

Instructions

1. Create an empty PICK Chart. If using with a group, use a whiteboard. If it's a personal PICK Chart, you can use a blank sheet of paper to draw a large PICK Chart or print a small chart using your computer. The chart should suit the size of the group that will use it.

2. The purpose of a PICK Chart is to decide which improvement ideas are most worthwhile to pursue based on expected profits and ease of implementation.

3. Write each idea on a sticky note. Place each sticky note into one of the four PICK Chart boxes.

4. Decide whether each idea is hard or easy to achieve. Think in terms of hours, manpower, expertise, and other factors that make implementing an idea difficult or easy.

5. Choose a payoff category. Determine if the improvement idea will result in a high or low payoff. *{When it comes to payoff category, factor in how this idea aligns with and brings you closer to fulfilling your purpose.}*

6. Place the sticky note with the idea written on it into the most suitable PICK Chart quadrant. Continue until all ideas have been placed in quadrants.

7. Choose {an idea or an opportunity} to act on based on their placement on the chart. Ideas that fall into the "Implement" category are the most worthwhile to pursue, followed by "Challenge" and "Possible." You should avoid **"Kill" ideas** *(unless Holy Spirit is compelling you to proceed.)*

Sample PICK Chart

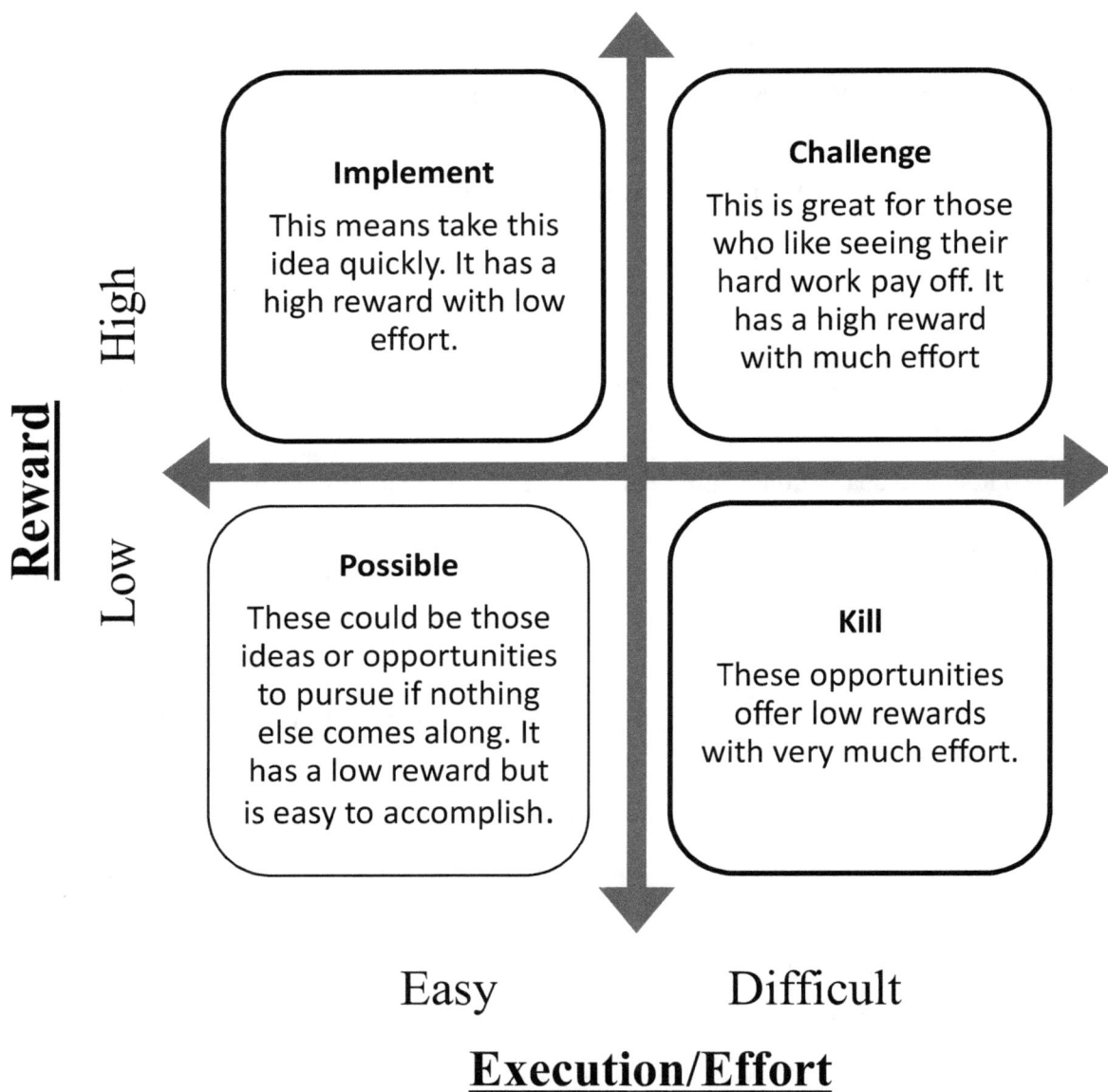

Implement
This means take this idea quickly. It has a high reward with low effort.

Challenge
This is great for those who like seeing their hard work pay off. It has a high reward with much effort

Possible
These could be those ideas or opportunities to pursue if nothing else comes along. It has a low reward but is easy to accomplish.

Kill
These opportunities offer low rewards with very much effort.

Reward — High / Low

Easy   Difficult

Execution/Effort

Blank PICK Chart

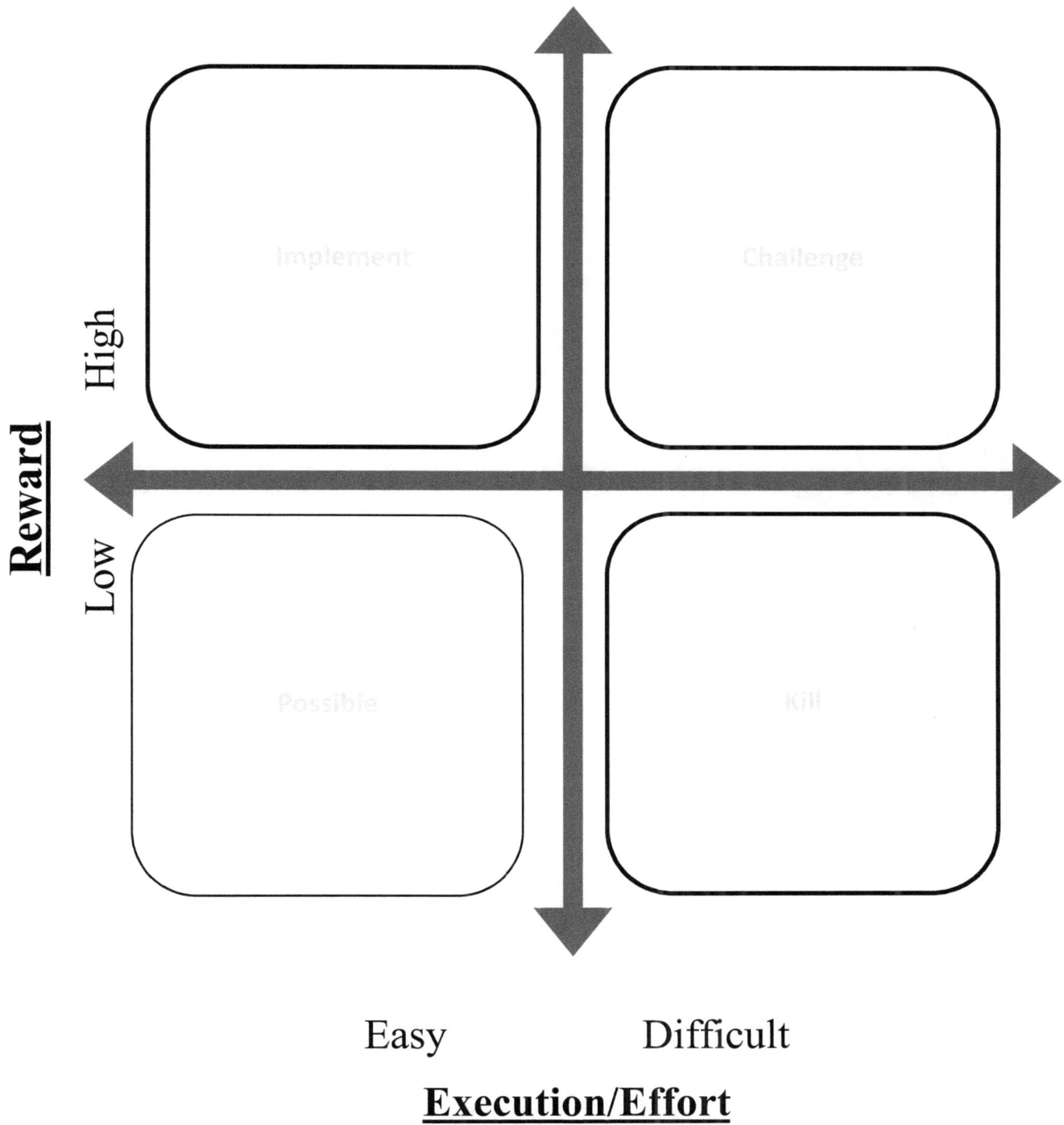

Implement

Challenge

High

Reward

Low

Possible

Kill

Easy   Difficult

Execution/Effort

About Coach Laura

Laura is the owner of the Serious Writers' Accountability Training (S.W.A.T.) Camp where authors create literary legacies and unleash their inner superhero through writing.

She leads 4-P Solutions Coaching, designed to help you: discover your purpose, realize your untapped potential, boost your productivity, and create sound plans for reaching your goals.

She is the founder and coach of Wells of Truth Peer-Based Bible Coaching Group. She teaches students how to study the Bible by using diverse and creative study techniques.

An Air Force veteran with a well-rounded view of modern-day issues, Laura's humor, wit, and creative delivery style keeps listeners engaged with the message and connected to the messenger. She has a "midwife's" heart and a gift for helping her audience discover, develop, and deliver their purpose and potential into the world.

Not one to shy away from taboo topics, Laura has been described as transparent, shocking, entertaining, and "raw"! Laura never fails to transform her audience's mindsets. She challenges them to conquer excuses and equips them with strategies for success to inspire them to live life with confidence and purpose.

Contact Coach Laura

www.coachlaurabrown.com

coachlaurabrown@gmail.com

Also Available on Amazon.com

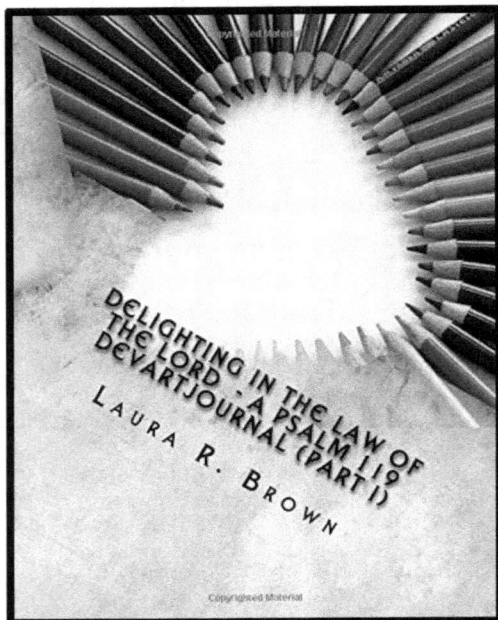

**Delighting in the Law of Lord
Psalm 119 Bible Study &
DevArtJournal**

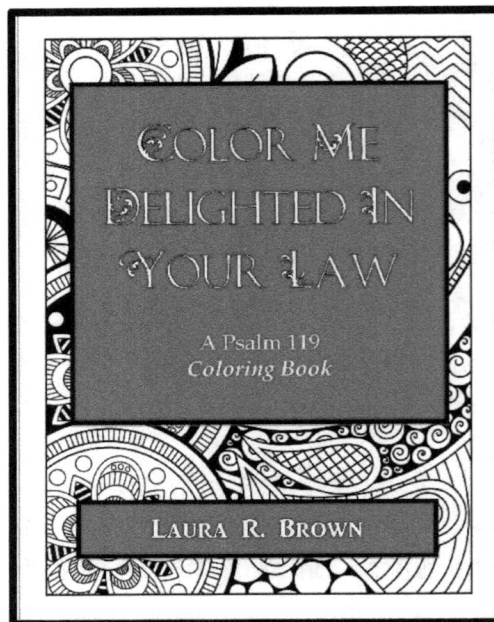

**Color Me Delighted in Your Law
A Psalm 119 Prayer Journal &
Coloring Book**

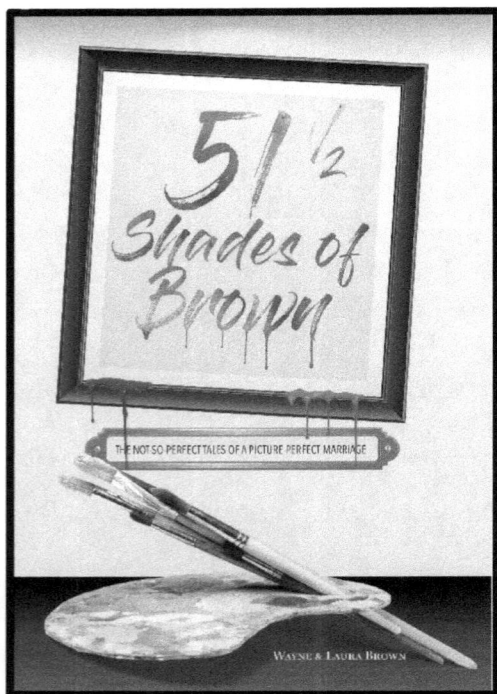

**51 ½ Shades of Brown
The Not-So-Perfect Tales of a
Picture-Perfect Marriage**

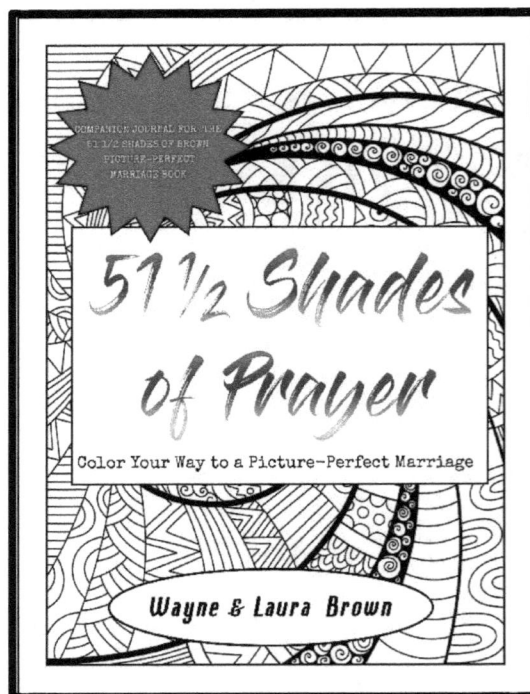

**51 ½ Shades of Prayer
Journal and Coloring Book**